THE ★JOHN WAYNE ULTIMATE PUZZLE BOOK

Media Lab Books
For inquiries, call 646-838-6637

Copyright 2017 Topix Media Lab

Published by Topix Media Lab
14 Wall Street, Suite 4B
New York, NY 10005

Printed in USA

ISBN 10: 1-942556-81-0
ISBN 13: 978-1942556-81-7

CEO Tony Romando

Vice President of Brand Marketing Joy Bomba   **Editor-in-Chief** Jeff Ashworth
Director of Finance Vandana Patel   **Creative Director** Steven Charny
Director of Sales and New Markets Tom Mifsud   **Photo Director** Dave Weiss
Manufacturing Director Nancy Puskuldjian   **Managing Editor** Courtney Kerrigan
Financial Analyst Matthew Quinn   **Senior Editor** Tim Baker
Brand Marketing Assistant Taylor Hamilton

Content Editors James Ellis, Kaytie Norman
Content Designer Michelle Lock
Art Director Susan Dazzo
Assistant Managing Editor Holland Baker
Designer Danielle Santucci
Assistant Photo Editors Catherine Armanasco, Jessica Ariel Wendroff
Assistant Editors Trevor Courneen, Alicia Kort
Editorial Assistants Mira Braneck, Brendan Luke,
Rachel Philips, Jordan Reisman

Co-Founders Bob Lee, Tony Romando

Cover: David Sutton/MPTV

TABLE OF CONTENTS

THE WORD SEARCHERS

If you're looking for words, these puzzles will accommodate ya.

THE WILD WEST

Duke made a whopping 83 Westerns in his 50-year film career.

```
O U M J S Z O R O Y C U S W Q R W C J F P N
R S P L H R P O M E V H W T O F A Q Z C X S
E K G J T L U H R Z O J U O A C L T T I W Q
D T U N A X K P R E N G S C L R T L T H D K
N C Q S H X F P S M K T F Q K Q U W S O Z Y
A F S F A L U T I N E C H Z G M O T P R M N
B O U S P C M L I R L E A S Q B O L R S S K
V D D E T B G A S V K Q P J U O D E A E B J
Z H E N I H S N O O M T C I H B L W I T O Z
L O N E S T A R E F L O M A E D M E R O V U
T E Y R Q P R E K O P V C U D B A A I J X R
O R E T O P N J C D E K H A V W A A E N A V
O U L Y K O Y D W G Z E S Q M D N L L R S O
B E H X D I J D C L G A G F Q T S U D W A S
Y K E V P X K G I D T E Y O N D E R S N C W
```

AMBUSH	HORSE	POKER
BANDERO	JACKEROO	PRAIRIE
BOOT	LASSO	ROOSTER
CAHOOTS	LONE STAR	SADDLE
CHUCK	MOONSHINE	SAWDUST
COLT	OUTLAW	SPURS
FALUTIN	PIEBALD	YONDER

Duke takes a break in his hotel room in London, 1951.

DUKE'S PERSONAL LIFE

His family, his pets, his favorite pastimes and more!

```
A R F F M Q V W X Y I J M T R Q X D U K E R
I H E Q O F A A E Q O S G R U A X R H N N N
N I X I R O D X U S I W A O Z R L C Q D J A
R U P O R N T R K T T A E P U D F I Y X W H
O T K Q I R K B O R N E P W U M Z H P O V T
F E O L S Y E I A T L F R E P A T R I C K E
I C E T O V R T O L R E M N Z E I X F C W F
L M N C N T N N E T L A A P D B O J I O Z E
A K X K A G I Q W L R A O H V F C H V W J X
C Q Q P Q A H H L I A Y K D C V I R Z B H A
Q O D X X C N E O B T D G U G I D I E O P S
A S I R A M D N W N K C E X Y S M O N Y I S
P X X H T P L G N S T A R R P V E O E K C I
E N I H P E S O J G N I H S I F I L N A P A
W I L D G O O S E L N Q S A F A X N X G A X
```

AIREDALE TERRIER
AISSA
CALIFORNIA
ANTONIA
COWBOY
DUKE
ETHAN
FISHING

FOOTBALL
IOWA
JOSEPHINE
MARION
MARISA
MELINDA
MICHAEL
MORRISON

NEWPORT
PATRICK
PATRIOTISM
PILAR
STAR
WESTERN
WILD GOOSE

FIGHTING FOR FREEDOM

"Out here, due process is a bullet!"
—John Wayne as Col. Mike Kirby in *The Green Berets* (1968)

```
Q W Z J N P A R P E S P Y D B A N R L C V L
V N J T Y F M A D P F L B B G W E W N B Q K
H P I F H O B A O Z X R F E O C T F S L S J
J R B H S F N O C N J R L D O R C A L N E I
F S T E R E B N E E R G D N V J L E R B A E
A G V D R D E G T D S N E V M U M R E D L T
T V Y G I O K D K N A A W G T D R M G Y T A
I N L R L P S I C T A B B E A Z O J I F E R
G F D M A B J U S F G N V D O W F X M E R E
U I G T B L L T P R D Y E E O H I D E V A B
E E R Z V M P C I E V U T T Y V N Q N O L I
S O S E V E T E R A N L W P U C U Z T Z F L
L G G D K T B A S I C K O V I E T N A M R Y
E G A L F U O M A C P R I W L R I O L O W X
F N P S K T O R T X O F Y G A C A L R R A G
```

BASE CAMP	GRENADE	SALUTE
BASIC	LIBERATE	SEAL
CAMOUFLAGE	LIEUTENANT	STAND DOWN
FATIGUES	PATROL	UNIFORM
FLARE	RECON	USO
FOXTROT	REGIMENT	VETERAN
GREEN BERETS	ROTC	VIETNAM

The Green Berets, 1968

John Wayne aboard the *Wild Goose* in the Mediterranean Sea, 1963.

OUT AT SEA

There was little John Wayne loved more than spending time on his boat, the *Wild Goose*.

```
R C X H B A B O F Q I X B T G H P Y P O R T
Q L I U B D Y W M D F I F U P U A H D H K R
U P O O Y U K H R L R N W O D N E T T A B S
D Y A M O H T A F L E Q P U R M D R C D P F
Y R T N F W O S Z A E H G E Z A T O S H U Z
D L A G Z B L F T U F N L X J O Y W E O N C
X X B O R W W O N Q C L O K N G L A F W S A
R C I A B F C I H S I Y D K C A C E H G W Z
N E T F G R A Y N T K C E D K N K S R U P Y
Z S D V Z F E S A D M T H Z R G H M I D N A
L H T D N T T V C T W M N A O W W F O C S C
E O M Z U M Z D O L X A M J T A M T Y Y H H
E L V U I R R I U N D E R W A Y C A B I N T
K B T A N U P N H F Q X A D N L J B F Z G H
L B C Q T H E I B G V C W V L P Q W L I O D
```

ABOARD	**HATCH**	**SEAWORTHY**
BATTEN DOWN	**HELM**	**SQUALL**
BUOY	**KEEL**	**STARBOARD**
CABIN	**KNOT**	**TILLER**
DECK	**OVERBOARD**	**UNDERWAY**
FATHOM	**PORT**	**WINDWARD**
GANGWAY	**RUDDER**	**YACHT**

PATRIOTISM

John Wayne's love for his country knew no bounds.

```
C A V A L R Y E C S L Y V D J N H C S T P M
Y E A G L E T R A O R J I C O K T O E N R T
E X T L K U Y M O E U G O I W M G U P A O R
Z Y K U L C E A V L N N T S S M N R I I U E
H Z C A B R Z A W I G U T G O C E A R L D D
G V S U I I R Z T G T D E R U X R G T A Y W
X N I C C B R Y N I V Y L Q Y X T E S V T H
C R A T W K J T T G Y Q J O G C S Y D K L I
U N E B X L L S V I N D E P E N D E N C E T
A V Z F Q O N M O D E E R F Y G B V A O D E
R E H E V O L I Y H W A C I R E M A S M L B
G V C O C S K Q C U F G J U Y G I I I R H Q L
Z F H U N F Y C A R C O M E D Q B Q A J G U
D Z E V U O C R X Y T S X W I J K O T A V E
L G T O P W R X N V E L U R Y J J J Y S K L G
```

AMERICANA
AMERICA, WHY I
  LOVE HER
BRAVERY
CAVALRY
CONSTITUTION
COUNTRY
COURAGE

DEMOCRACY
DIGNITY
EAGLE
FREEDOM
HONOR
INDEPENDENCE
OLD GLORY
PROUD

RED, WHITE, BLUE
SALUTE
STARS AND
  STRIPES
STRENGTH
TRIBUTE
VALIANT

GUEST STAR

Search out the names of the TV shows on which Duke
guest starred in this word search.

```
W O H S N I T R A M N A E D E H T K Q Q C C
E T U L A S W C H Z B W E Z R P I Q N T L A
N I A R T N O G A W Z R Q D E G L Z T G I S
T E X A C O S T A R T H E A T R E R G O M A
T H E D I C K P O W E L L T H E A T R E A B
K V A V G T H E B O B H O P E S H O W N X L
R U O H N O T L E K S D E R E H T H Z W S A
R O W A N A N D M A R T I N S L A U G H I N
S E I L L I B L L I H Y L R E V E B E H T C
E F I L R U O Y S I S I H T M A U D E D O A
A L C O A P R E M I E R E I L O V E L U C Y
D L R O W E D I W E D I W N O S N I K R A P
W H A T S M Y L I N E G U N S M O K E X F U
L H Q F D T H E E D S U L L I V A N S H O W
L W O H S S A L G U O D E K I M E H T M Y T
```

ALCOA PREMIERE
CASABLANCA
CLIMAX!
GUNSMOKE
I LOVE LUCY
MAUDE
PARKINSON
ROWAN & MARTIN'S
   LAUGH-IN
SALUTE

TEXACO STAR
   THEATRE
THE BEVERLY
   HILLBILLIES
THE BOB HOPE SHOW
THE DEAN MARTIN
   SHOW
THE DICK POWELL
   THEATRE

THE ED SULLIVAN
   SHOW
THE MIKE DOUGLAS
   SHOW
THE RED SKELTON
   HOUR
THIS IS YOUR LIFE
WAGON TRAIN
WHAT'S MY LINE
WIDE WIDE WORLD

Duke with Goldie Hawn on *Rowan and Martin's Laugh-In*, 1972

MOVIE MAGIC

Duke made movies for 50 years, turning him into
an international star and American legend.

```
S C E N E R Y E M G W N W Q C A K E Z B M A
Q H B K B B G H O N A E T H E B M R W O H F
W U S E N G E X V Z U U S F H T L U F X N J
W F O Z S R Z M H N L T R T S D I T I O T A
T W W T O O L I M D S L E O E L F R L F P P
A C A D E M Y A W A R D S C T R B E M F L X
X A M I L C C T R E E E Z H A N V P I D X
E S O L I L Q E C A P P V Y L N R O V C M T
Q M J N A R D U D G O V S U H E I R O E A Z
W W E M C C D E G Z F R L M L S U C A H C H
J M A L A O X H R O T C E R I D C Q O N T E
A R X R R Z I Y U A C D V C K T V D E L I P
D J P P J P K X H E R H N Q D M S D P S O Q
V E I Z W F G E N R E D A E L F J T P Z N R
T H N Z D I F R V Y H Z S O I R L V A E H I
```

ACADEMY
   AWARDS
ACTION
B FILM
BOX OFFICE
CINEMA
CLIMAX

DIRECTOR
DRAMA
FILM
GENRE
HERO
LEAD
NARRATOR
OVERTURE

PRODUCER
QUOTE
RED CARPET
SCENERY
SEQUEL
TECHNICOLOR
WESTERN

Director John Wayne on the set of *The Alamo*, 1960.

The Big Trail, 1930

DUKE IN THE '30S

John Wayne appeared in more than 70 movies during the 1930s—
see if you can find some of them!

```
S M V T U I S T E X A S C Y C L O N E T Y T
R A A H H T N E G D N A Y D A L W H B H E H
E K G T H E B I G T R A I L E C I V A R L E
L E K I N G O F T H E P E C O S N D T E L D
I R Z E G X C R L Z R K N S E V V W O E A A
O O E V P L Z E E O S A J S V E O C H G V W
P F R G I S E Y R G M V T K N F O B D I W N
S M I W Z T H R P O O A N T I N C A R R O R
A E K K S A E D R Y G N U S F E X B A L B I
E N B E I T R H Q E G R T L V F G Y W S N D
S D U L S U G K C E E E I R B W S F T L I E
D L W A Y U G O I S D C X X A G R A S O A R
B B X G O F A H E L T C O A X I G C E S R L
R E G R P C Q N A N O Z I R A W L E W T T C
T F B O H T D W T S E W E H T O T N R O B H
```

ADVENTURE'S END
ARIZONA
BABY FACE
BLUE STEEL
BORN TO THE WEST
CONFLICT
KING OF THE PECOS

LADY AND GENT
MAKER OF MEN
RAINBOW VALLEY
ROUGH ROMANCE
SEA SPOILERS
STAGECOACH
TEXAS CYCLONE

TEXAS TERROR
THE BIG TRAIL
THE DAWN RIDER
THE OREGON TRAIL
THREE GIRLS LOST
TWO-FISTED LAW
WESTWARD HO

DUKE IN THE '40S

After 1939's *Stagecoach*, Duke was well on his way
to becoming a household name by starring in these classics.

```
W I T H O U T R E S E R V A T I O N S R E I
E C N A R F N I N O I N U E R G Y D A E L N
T H E S P O I L E R S J D K N F J N M A D O
R E D R I V E R O H Y G S P X O A A I P D L
T H G I N A R O F Y D A L T U R P M J T A D
A M A N B E T R A Y E D J M G T K M O H S O
A N G E L A N D T H E B A D M A N O W E E K
N M C Q Y K C J N P C V Z X J P O C I W H L
T H R E E F A C E S W E S T S A O K F I T A
N A A T A B O T K C A B N T L C C R O L N H
H G R U B S T T I P Y U M E O H Y A S D I O
V W X B P A B R Q N Y E X P P E T D D W L M
E L B A D N E P X E E R E W Y E H T N I L A
S R E N N I S N E V E S A T O K A D A N A X
W S F L Y I N G T I G E R S H S Z Q S D T U
```

A MAN BETRAYED	RED RIVER
ANGEL AND THE BADMAN	REUNION IN FRANCE
BACK TO BATAAN	SANDS OF IWO JIMA
DAKOTA	SEVEN SINNERS
DARK COMMAND	TALL IN THE SADDLE
FLYING TIGERS	THE SPOILERS
FORT APACHE	THEY WERE EXPENDABLE
IN OLD OKLAHOMA	THREE FACES WEST
LADY FOR A NIGHT	TYCOON
PITTSBURGH	WITHOUT RESERVATIONS
REAP THE WILD WIND	

Tycoon, 1947

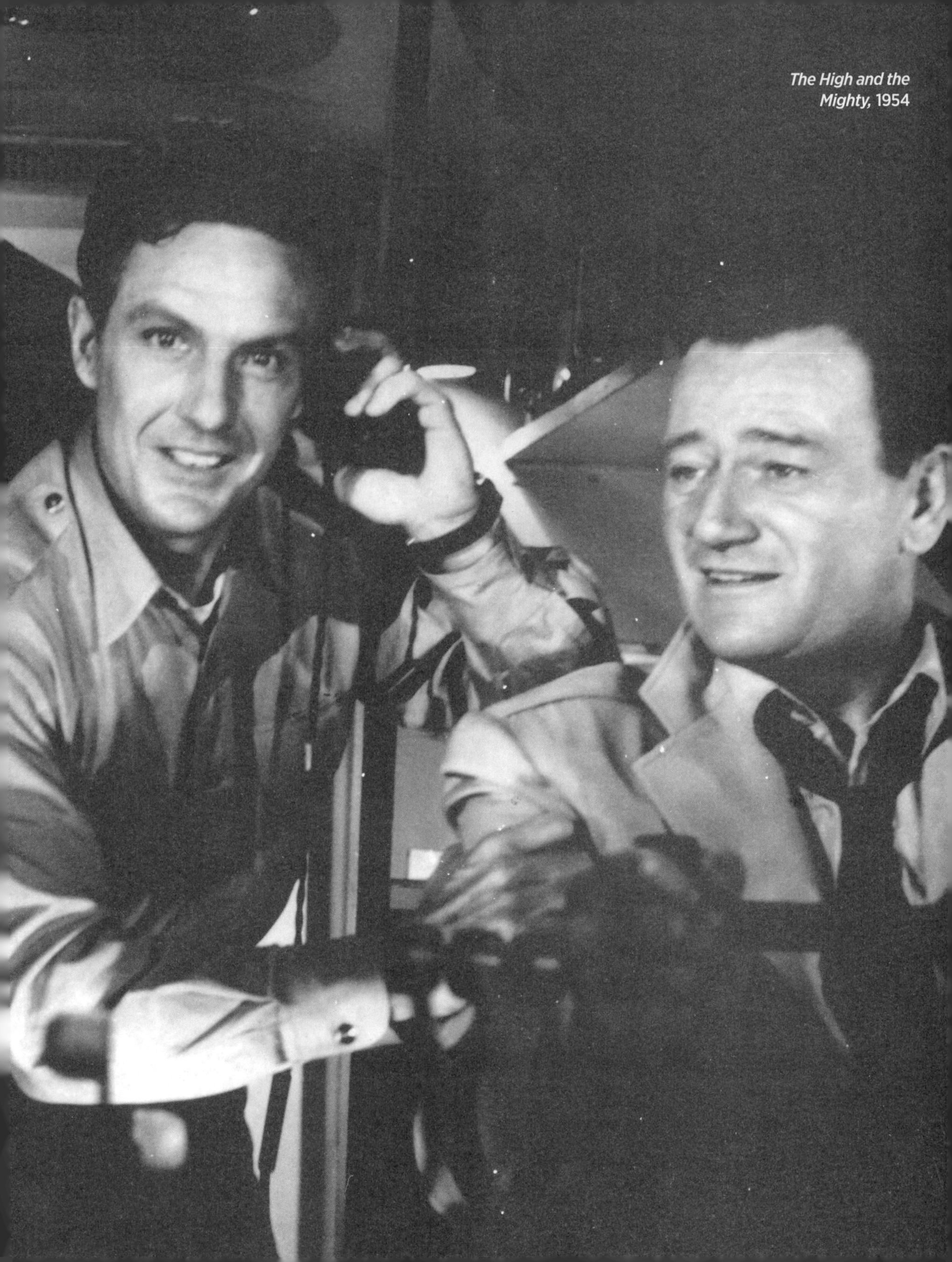

The High and the Mighty, 1954

DUKE IN THE '50S

John Wayne's fourth decade of filmmaking brought us
unforgettable fare such as *Rio Grande* and *The Searchers*.

```
O D N O H B T S O L E H T F O D N E G E L T
S R E H C R A E S E H T Y E L L A D O O L B
X E P D W V Y M I P Q L F J E T P I L O T N
N A I R A B R A B E H T N P P T G G K T J A
Y A W E H T G N O L A E L B U O R T I H L M
R C Y K O N S R E I D L O S E S R O H E H T
Y T H G I M E H T D N A H G I H E H T C E E
H K N I M A R R I E D A W O M A N W R O D I
B I G J I M M C L A I N Z M G D Y O I N N U
J X N M Z F S Y Q O Y Q P N Q A H F O Q A Q
M W X H S T H E S E A C H A S E H N B U R E
F L Y I N G L E A T H E R N E C K S R E G H
O P E R A T I O N P A C I F I C Y Q A R O T
F Y K S E H T N I D N A L S I C L M V O I Q
T H E W I N G S O F E A G L E S D T O R R O
```

BIG JIM MCLAIN
BLOOD ALLEY
FLYING LEATHERNECKS
HONDO
I MARRIED A WOMAN
ISLAND IN THE SKY
JET PILOT
LEGEND OF THE LOST
RIO GRANDE
OPERATION PACIFIC

THE BARBARIAN (AND THE GEISHA)
THE CONQUEROR
THE HIGH AND THE MIGHTY
THE HORSE SOLDIERS
THE QUIET MAN
THE SEA CHASE
THE SEARCHERS
THE WINGS OF EAGLES
TROUBLE ALONG THE WAY
RIO BRAVO

DUKE IN THE '60S

Duke hardly slowed down in the next decade,
earning an Oscar for his work in *True Grit* (1969).

```
Y P T A L K Q H A T A R I S Q E R E L T D T
X M Q N O R T H T O A L A S K A M J R H R H
C S P G D G A D O N O V A N S R E E F E A E
G R E A T E S T S T O R Y E V E R T O L D C
S H O T L I B E R T Y V A L A N C E E O L O
N S R E T H G I F L L E H G J E R R U N R M
R E D L E E I T A K F O S N O S E H T G O A
Y I D J S T M C L I N T O C K T L G I E W N
H O W T H E W E S T W A S W O N D F R S S C
S T E R E B N E E R G E H T B W O X G T U H
M X M D E T A E F E D N U E H T R A E D C E
Q F O E G H X N H F E P I J F S A Y U A R R
W O D A H S T N A I G A T S A C D D R Y I O
H T H E W A R W A G O N F F H I O U T Y C S
Y A W S M R A H N I O M A L A E H T I D W N
```

CAST A GIANT SHADOW
CIRCUS WORLD
DONOVAN'S REEF
EL DORADO
HATARI!
HELLFIGHTERS
HOW THE WEST WAS WON
IN HARM'S WAY
MCLINTOCK
NORTH TO ALASKA

THE ALAMO
THE COMANCHEROS
(THE) GREATEST STORY EVER TOLD
THE GREEN BERETS
THE LONGEST DAY
(THE MAN WHO) SHOT LIBERTY VALANCE
THE SONS OF KATIE ELDER
THE UNDEFEATED
THE WAR WAGON
TRUE GRIT

THE MAN WHO SHOT LIBERTY VALANCE

"When the legend becomes fact, print the legend." —Carleton Young as reporter
Maxwell Scott, *The Man Who Shot Liberty Valance* (1962)

```
F L A S H B A C K R N D O O H E T A T S H R
T X Y H X O L T Y E O B C M V Q E F L C T Q
F R K V T B M Z E I H L G R S E U D A O S T
S M A M D P L E I T P M E O O N V O G A R M
S E C W V C C L L N I I A E E T C K C P U F
X O L C E X N Y L O N O W R M E A R N T L K
W B E I C T I N A R O K A V G A I N H U E F
G N G J M H S E H F D L S A I F R G E D O S
R E H C N A R S Q P M L T H I K I V N S F T
J O H N F O R D E V O S R C I F M E I T L O
P O M P E Y V E Y M T W E A N N G T G N A D
A U G Q L W F O V T A A P U A E B P Y S W D
J X K K X J W X F H W J G P L F P O J C X A
A R V G R X N B W X E L Z Z C L V E N M S R
E C N A L A V Y T R E B I L F U U R O E X D
```

FLASHBACK	LEE MARVIN	SENATOR
FRONTIER	LEGEND	SHINBONE
FUNERAL	LIBERTY VALANCE	STAGECOACH
GUNFIGHT	POMPEY	STATEHOOD
HALLIE	RANCHER	STODDARD
JOHN FORD	RULE OF LAW	TOM DONIPHON
JAMES STEWART	SACRIFICE	VERA MILES

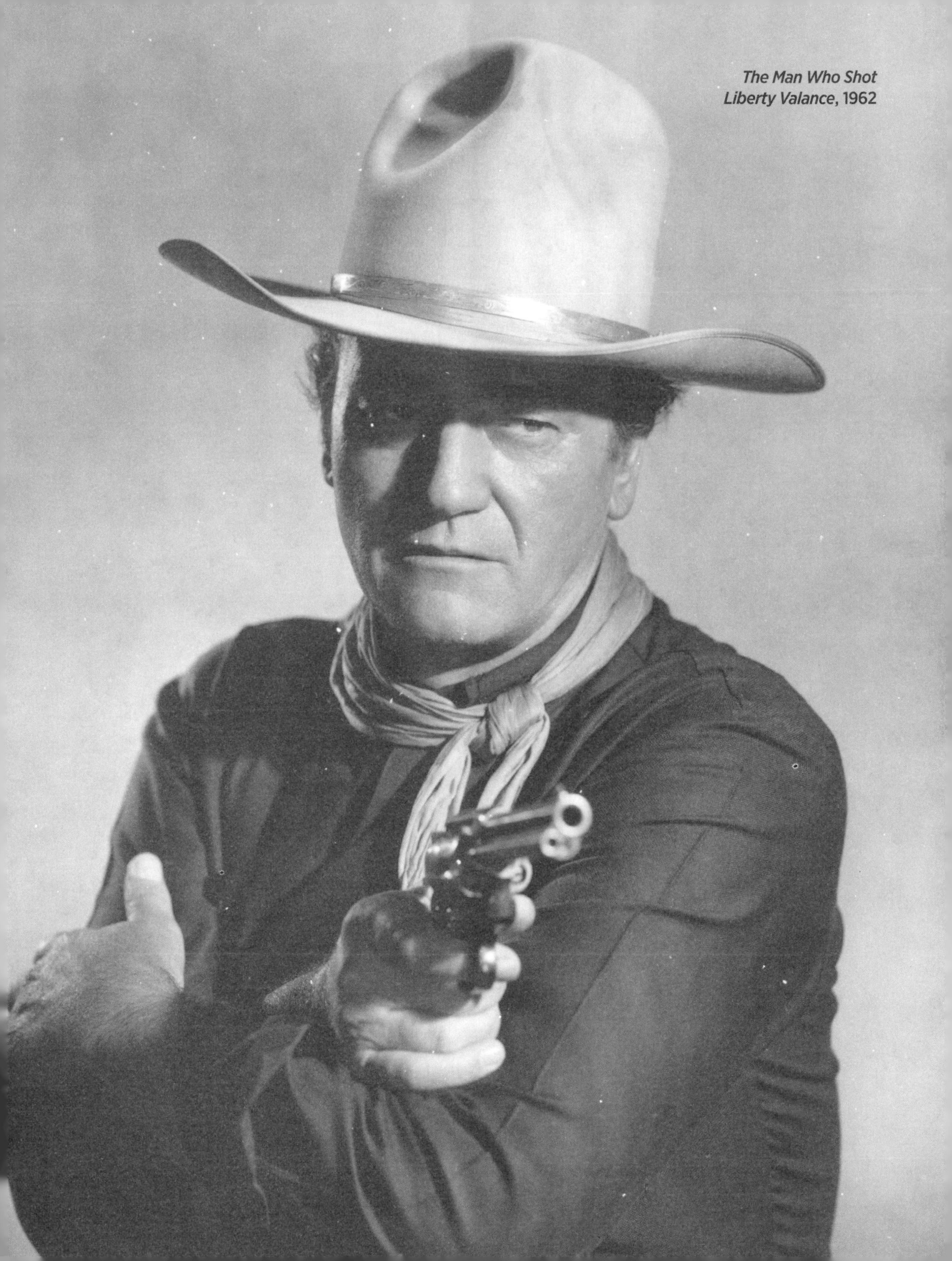

The Man Who Shot Liberty Valance, 1962

Big Jake, 1971

BIG JAKE

This film involved John Wayne's three sons: Patrick and Ethan had roles as
Big Jake's son and grandson and Michael was the producer.

```
E F L N A Y O J Y C N J T J Y X J A Y M P E
H B J T A C F Y U V P O C P K A O R C P Q K
C X D N I M T W I E T E H C A M H A Y S O A
A U I X R G R G I S V B G Y H R N H P S O J
P T E Z B X R E M E D R S U K A F O A R G E
A M S R E T O O H S P R A H S N A N T E U L
M C C A N D L E S S G L Y R J S I E R G N T
C H I L L I C O T H E C A N Y O N E I N F T
E T H A N W A Y N E S G A L W M X R C A I I
G N I P P A N D I K E U R V J P T U K R G L
J Z B S X S J N J V R P B O U T L A W S H E
S R A L L O D N O I L L I M E N O M A A T K
B R R I C H A R D B O O N E A G S T Y X E K
Q W M B O B O O V M U H W M H G V K N E R N
Q L J L U N G O T P K R R K O P T O E T W M
```

AMBUSH
APACHE
CANYON
CHILLICOTHE
DOG
ETHAN WAYNE
GEORGE SHERMAN
GUNFIGHTER

JOHN FAIN
KIDNAPPING
LITTLE JAKE
MACHETE
MAUREEN O'HARA
MCCANDLES
MEXICO

ONE MILLION
  DOLLARS
OUTLAW
PATRICK WAYNE
RANSOM
RICHARD BOONE
SHARP SHOOTER
TEXAS RANGERS

RIO LOBO

"I've been called a lot of things, but not 'comfortable!'"
—John Wayne as Col. Cord McNally, *Rio Lobo* (1970)

```
S C T T A L S T K T R Y H T N J Y E S Z A W
F E D E W T B H U K L R O N I P G A J N M T
H X T E C C I S E L E X S E C M X H O Y Q S
K J H A B H C L A R M U D R M E O D V N A G
A F J G R A N N E Y I U U E T T R W E H R K
A D L L R E C I U M D F T G Y O L E S E I Z
L S B O Y M D A C C A D F I C X E S R N G X
A N R U D M U E T O T R F L S P N T O D N W
O A Q R R O C I F S L W A L T U O E H R H V
X G O U Z Y U K R N A O L E P L L R Q I R U
E C K E T C H A M P O H R B R O O N J C B Q
H O W A R D H A W K S C S L R K C A P K V X
S P I L L I H P N A M D L O Y V C F B S X Y
T R L K U Y W R A W L I V I C K N J R R M G
N L G C X B Q Q K G W O G N G E U N I O N G
```

AMELITA	HENDRICKS	SHASTA
BELLIGERENT	HIJACK	SHERIFF
CIVIL WAR	HORSE	TECHNICOLOR
COLONEL	HOWARD HAWKS	TEXAS
CONFEDERATES	KETCHAM	TUSCARORA
CORD MCNALLY	OLD MAN PHILLIPS	UNION
CORDONA	OUTLAW	WESTERN

Rio Lobo, 1970

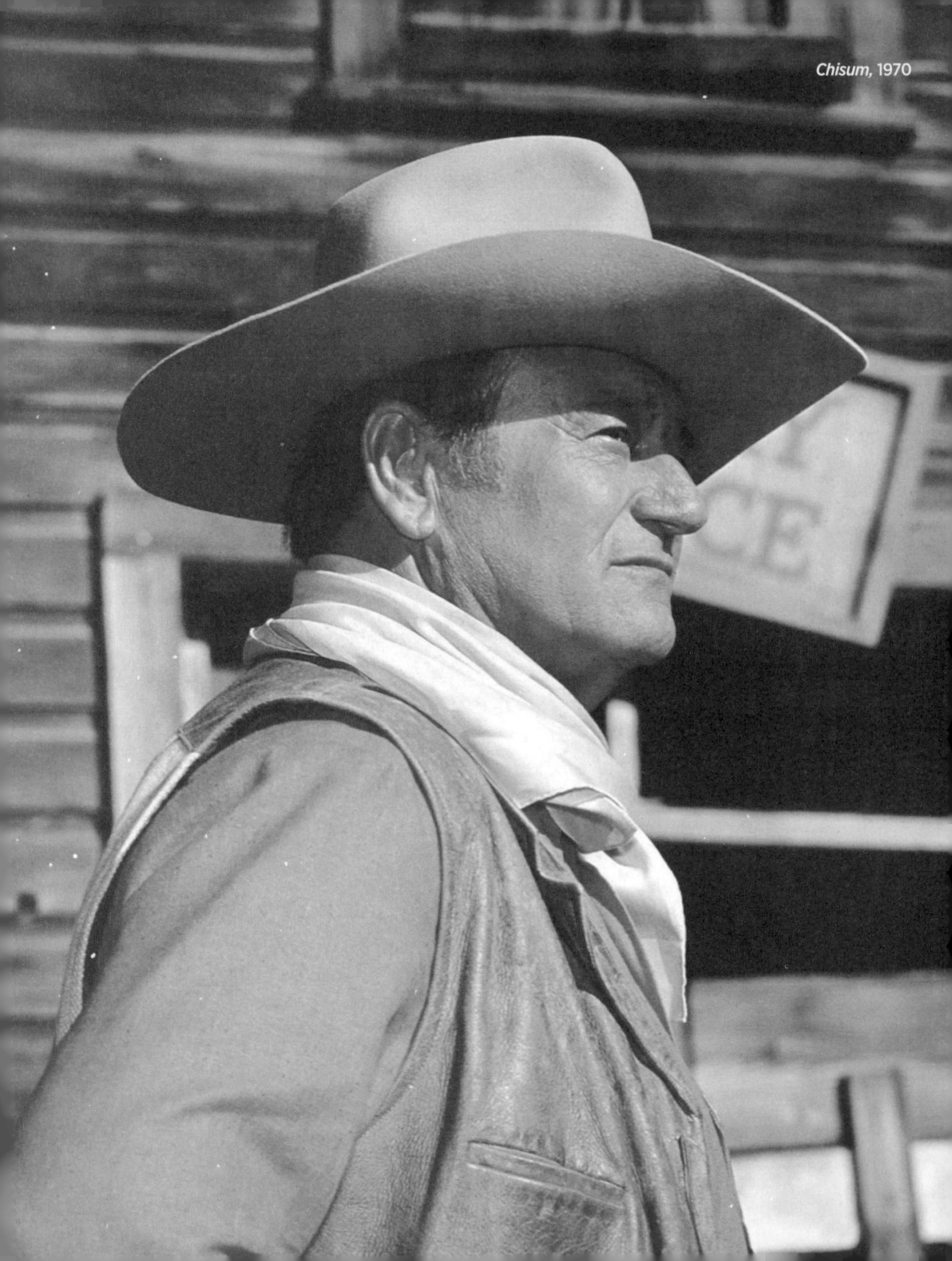

Chisum, 1970

CHISUM

"We may have to be neighbors, but I don't have to be neighborly."
—John Wayne as John Simpson Chisum, *Chisum* (1970)

```
R A W Y T N U O C N L O C N I L M X F R Y G
E F A T N A S E E Q A S L M P Q M N F E H E
S Y S C W D I U O Z D M I I M U M E I V P N
L E C F O N G W M H L B S Q S T H E R E R E
A L Y R O T I R R E T O C I X E M W E N U R
B L O U Y D Z W A J H F H J H T R S H G M A
B A T J A C P R O D U C T I O N S C S E E L
U V E C I T S U J S N D E P U T Y M T P C S
N S G R N A E O F H N N Y P D P S W A E N T
O O S L Q J A P O I I G Q N J X S V M P E O
F C O P D V D J E I L L A S A V W P P P R R
H E N R Y T U N S T A L L I W M A J E E W E
N P G M R R L D I K E H T Y L L I B D R A X
O U G H C E E N T L R A N C H E R T E B L H
F I S T F I G H T N H D E P B F E E E Y B F
```

BATJAC PRODUCTIONS
BILLY THE KID
DEPUTY
DYNAMITE
FIST FIGHT
GENERAL STORE
HENRY TUNSTALL

JOHN CHISUM
JUSTICE
LAWRENCE MURPHY
LINCOLN COUNTY WAR
MCSWEEN
NEW MEXICO
 TERRITORY
PECOS VALLEY

PEPPER
RANCHER
REVENGE
SALLIE
SANTA FE
SHERIFF
STAMPEDE

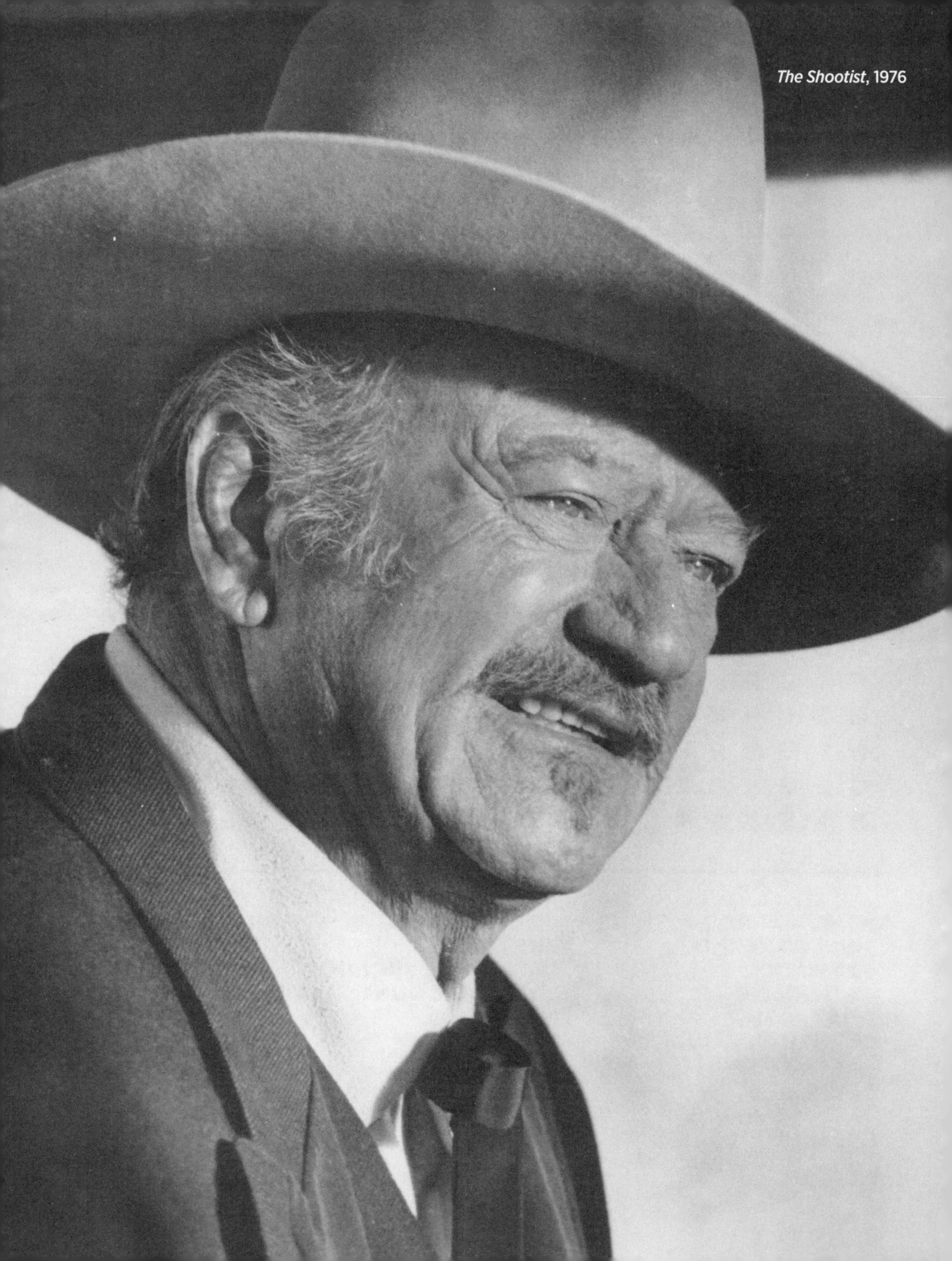

The Shootist, 1976

THE SHOOTIST

See if you can find all the words related to Duke's final film.

```
A J Z E K J O Y L G L V E B N S N N N G D C
R G A S G D D A F V A S K I R K W U E D T D
R E R M I A U Q L V U P X R D O O W V O I J
V C G B E D R E N O R A X T L O R B A J N N
X E I N A S G U H U E N U H E B B E D I R P
C H N N I E S G O W N L K D Q B S D A A X S
T A U G I L N T A C B M G A E J E Q O Y Y M
Q M N S E I S Y E I A J Y Y M H S H Y B R G
A C N C D A L N Z W C I T U O T O O H S U T
E O R R E A N O U P A P V B P Q M G Q F G B
D I A G Y R K C J G L R N R O N H O W A R D
P O L D W E S T E V L W T Y R Q W R G E G N
B T E N O O B D R A H C I R T P I O A W K Z
M A R S H A L W A L T E R T H I B I D O K H
U M S F S B G N O O L A S E L O P O R T E M
```

BIRTHDAY
BOARDING HOUSE
CANCER
COURAGE
DON SIEGEL
GUNSLINGER
JAMES STEWART

J.B. BOOKS
LAUDANUM
LAUREN BACALL
MARSHAL WALTER
 THIBIDO
METROPOLE SALOON
MOSES BROWN
NEVADA

OLD WEST
PRIDE
RICHARD BOONE
RON HOWARD
SHOOTOUT
VENGEANCE
WAYLAY

The Longest Day, 1962

THE LONGEST DAY

This epic war film is based on the D-Day landings in Normandy on June 6, 1944.

```
K S R A D N O F Y R N E H T K U S E E H I B
E C E I A H T O P T S W M B P N I D G C I X
A V A I C E A A O R E U R Y A S Y D D N P C
E M B T L H U R H I H I A M E A F A I E X V
F N A F T L A B K C O E R N S N R Y R R W L
F O K R A A A R T T T E H X E W T E B F H Y
A R A N D F R I D U G O A L A N I J S R H E
W M K X S U M E H T W P O I N T E D U H O C
T A B B I T C C T E O H K E C N Q J S Q E W
F N I C R S A O R N I D D T O M O R A Q J J
U D B E F R T C D K U W D A N Z A L G B P G
L Y B X A U M V V D J O Q N N X X V E Z Q O
L O S P A M E R I C A N C F E W T F P K N O
R E G A T O B A S B E A C H R Z A A B R L M
S P B T W K F T R Z N W O V Y Y B O F T U F
```

ALLIES	EISENHOWER	PAUL ANKA
AMERICAN	FRENCH	PEGASUS BRIDGE
AXIS	GERMAN	POINTE DU HOC
BEACH	HENRY FONDA	RICHARD TODD
COUNTERATTACK	LUFTWAFFE	ROBERT MITCHUM
D-DAY	NORMANDY	SABOTAGE
DOCUDRAMA	PARACHUTE	SEAN CONNERY

THE QUIET MAN

This 1952 comedy-drama was nominated for Best Picture, proving Duke could shine as something other than a cowboy or military hero.

```
E D I S Y R T N U O C E S W W B E W C E T N
C R Q F N Y I H D R N V I W A R N N R N R Q
K I E I J R S R G Y E D O R R B Y R R Y O V
D C A V E A O E A I O X R X D W A S F A O Y
Y R N L E F R W A W F Y O H B Y W W A W P S
T P A P N R L A T N F T D B O R I O K A E E
U N B H Z E E I H I T N S O N W N P A D R P
D D O L A Y L N T O Q H P I D O O U E N T N
Q J Q H T L S Z D P N O O Z F D T E B I H Y
W R C H A G G A G R U E P R D I M W M L O B
D I O N X E R S S X J A E Z N O H S R E R Q
M V E D R N E L G A L C M R O T C I V M N N
U L P A T R I C K W A Y N E U C O L E K E N
B I L M A R Y K A T E V P A F A K N P A N R
L D C W G D Z G N I D D E W M R M C G H P T
```

BARRY
  FITZGERALD
BOXER
COUNTRYSIDE
DOWRY
FIST FIGHT
IRELAND

JOHN FORD
MARY KATE
MAUREEN O'HARA
MELINDA WAYNE
MICHAEL WAYNE
PATRICK WAYNE
REVEREND
SEAN THORNTON

TONI WAYNE
TRAIN
TROOPER THORN
VICTOR MCLAGLEN
WARD BOND
WEDDING
WIDOW TILLANE

Rio Bravo, 1959

RIO BRAVO

"Sorry don't get it done, Dude."
—John Wayne as Sheriff John T. Chance, *Rio Bravo* (1959)

```
O H Z Q N R G J A S F E U P F N Y S R H F P
S H U W E I N S P N M F K K S W T G E O E O
D Z X D M B T I X E G C I L K O U D T W A K
X Y R Y M M T R M V D I R R O T P G H A T E
X U N V C T D O A H X I E B E K E Z G R H R
M O R A O U Z D G M C A Y D T H D P I D E S
K G I O M E D U D K N D H E I C S H F H R L
R U N Z F I X M Y Z D A X S D C N Y N A S D
O W J U H C T N Q U I A E U T I K Q U W D U
F Z R V K S E E M R S M U D R U U I G K P M
M Y R I F L E M Y P O N Y A N D M E N S S K
R L L V S R O L O C I N H C E T V P Z S C L
Q W P O R E H C N A R J N O D J C L Y P O S
F W N C A R D C H E A T N U R S J K T X R N
V N T Z T S A L O O N S Q K Q R X B I U H H
```

ANGIE DICKINSON	GUNFIGHTER	RICKY NELSON
CARD CHEAT	HOWARD HAWKS	SALOON
DEAN MARTIN	MUDDY BOOTS	SHERIFF
DEPUTY	MURDER	SPITTOON
DUDE	MY RIFLE, MY PONY,	STUMPY
DYNAMITE	AND ME	TECHNICOLOR
FEATHERS	POKER	TEXAS
	RANCHER	

SHE WORE A YELLOW RIBBON

This 1949 Western won an Academy Award for Best Cinematography.

```
C F V Q E J M E H L D E A X D T J V N B N R
A E V X R Z O R G R I V N R K O G O V E Q J
V I E G H J N R N D E E O N A P I N V O U Y
A H T F T X U S P D I F U N E T F E U R I E
L C R E S T M A O L N R N T A Y R K O A N R
R E V G I R E Y R H K E D V E A E F X G C A
Y K T E W R N P O A D X R N P N F H G A A C
B F P J F M T J P R P E J O A I A X C N N Y
R E T S U C V W U P S A L F C D L N V H N R
Q X S F F Z A E G E H O H E T D S O T O O R
P P R Y P N L O R U G B R O M V T S R J N A
X W F L S B L G Q I S T A M P E D E I T N H
V N D D V X E B Z F O R T S T A R K E M A N
N W J E C O Y E N R O H G I B E L T T I L P
J K Z M W D J C G M W B S E L T T I R B A J
```

ARAPAHO	HARRY CAREY JR	MONUMENT VALLEY
BRITTLES	JOANNE DRU	NEVER APOLOGIZE
CAVALRY	JOHN AGAR	OFFICER
CHEYENNE	JOHN FORD	PATROL
CHIEF	LIEUTENANT	QUINCANNON
CUSTER	LITTLE BIG HORN	RESERVATION
FORT STARKE	MISS DANDRIDGE	STAMPEDE

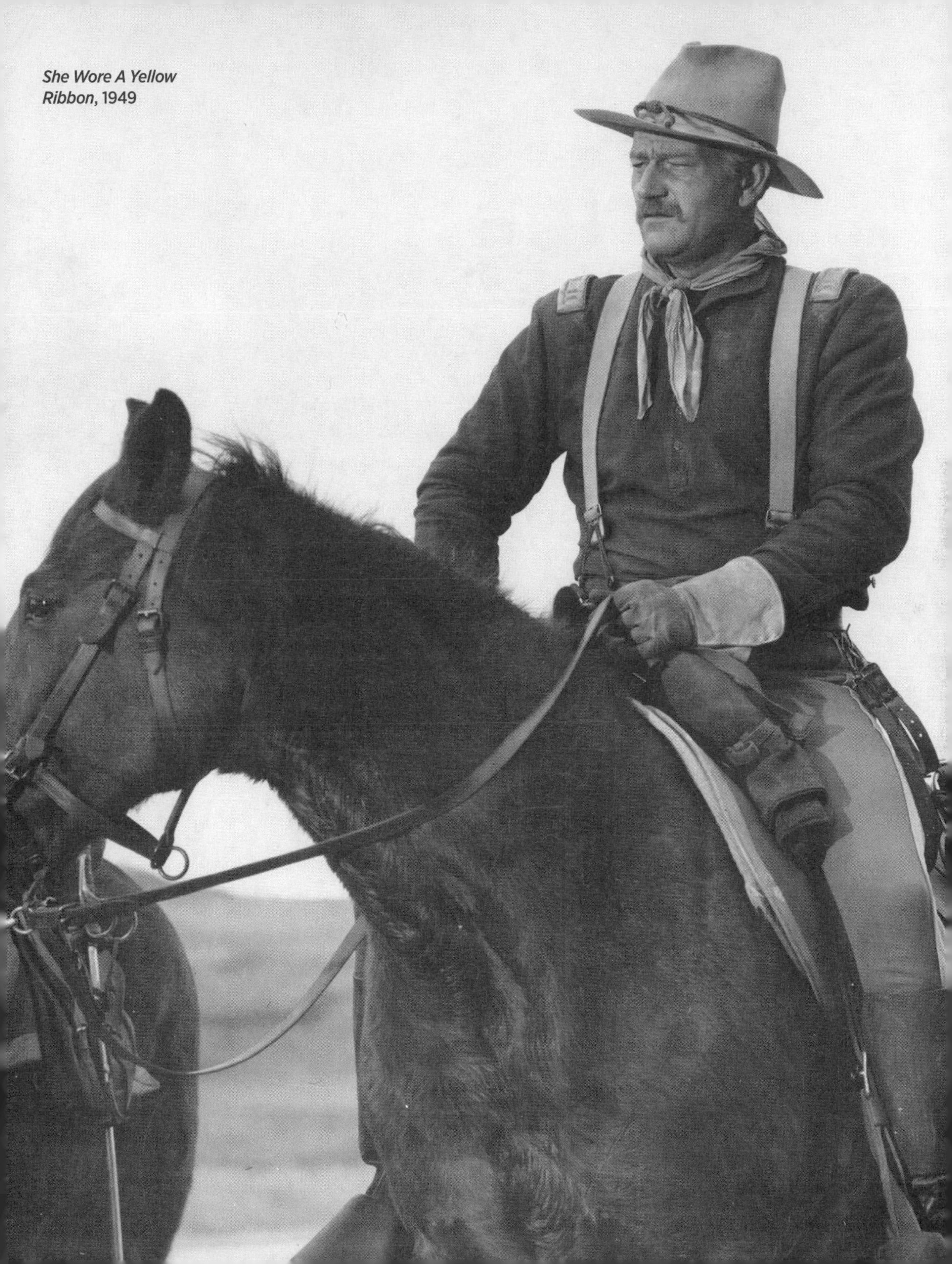

She Wore A Yellow Ribbon, 1949

JUSTICE JUMBLES

Unscramble each word, and then put them in the proper order to figure out the John Wayne quote.

HINT:

This quote is from *The Green Berets*.

1. CRPOESS

2. UBLTLE

3. SI

4. UOT

5. UDE

6. RHEE

The Green Berets, 1968

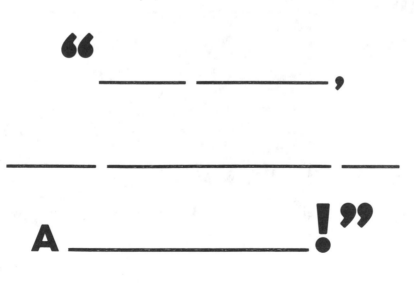

" _____ _____,

_____ _____ ___

A _____ !"

HINT:

John Wayne said this while making *The Shootist*.

1. CGHANE

2. ICPTUESR

3. VEOR

4. UYG

5. VAHE

6. TSHO

7. NI

8. V'IE

9. ACBK

10. AMED

11. ADN

12. TI

13. RVNEE

14. HET

" _____ _____

_____ 250

_____ _____

_____ _____

A _____ _____

_____ _____.

_____ __. "

The Shootist,
1976

True Grit, 1969

HINT:
This quote is from *True Grit*.

1. **AELFL**

2. **FI**

3. **ROF**

4. **OLOKGIN**

5. **UNOYG**

6. **O'UYER**

7. **AY**

8. **LI'L**

9. **TMMOCODAAEC**

10. **TOBULER**

" _____ _____ , _____
_____ _____
_____ _____ , _____
_____ _____ . "

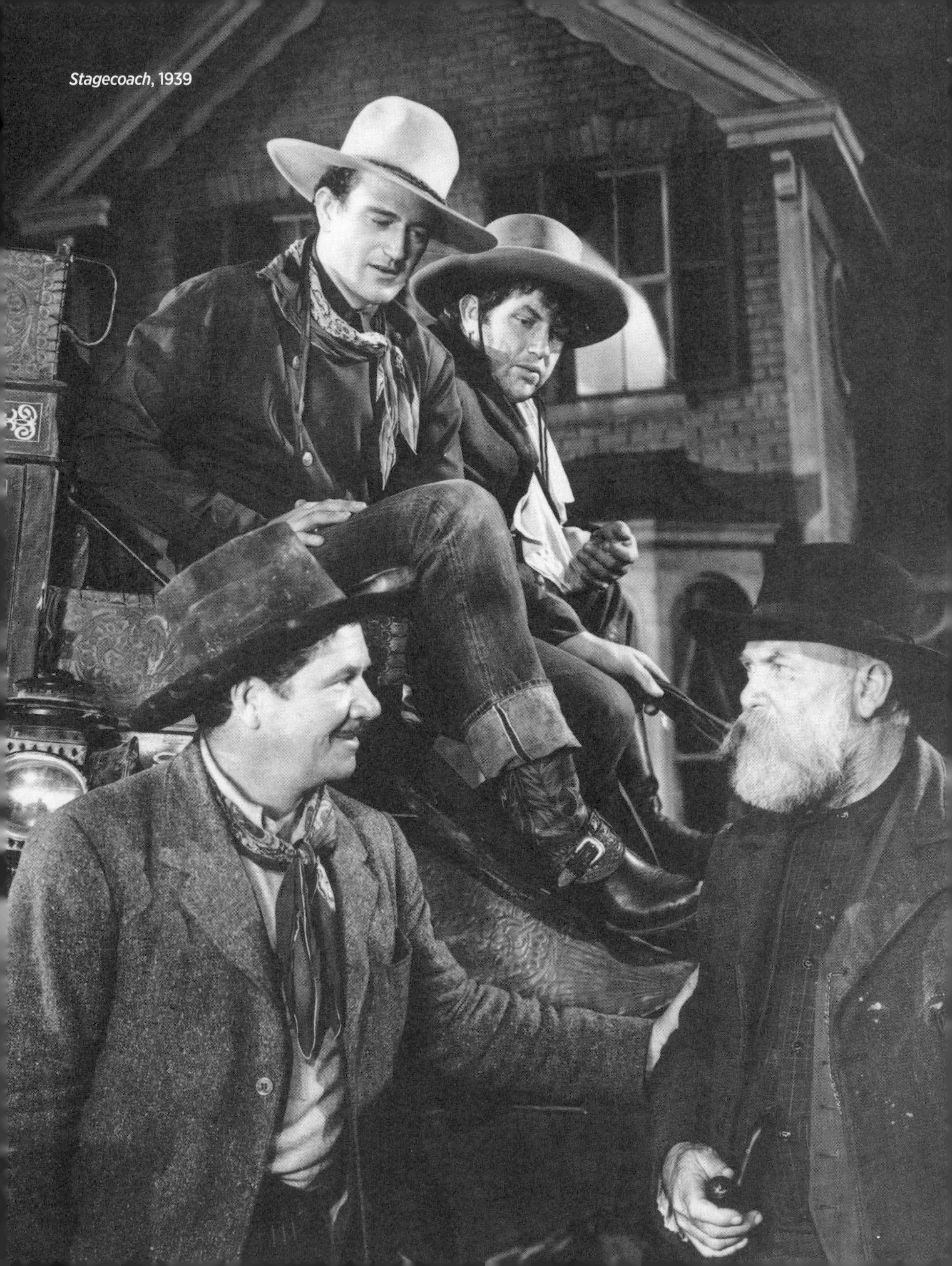

Stagecoach, 1939

HINT:

This quote is from *Stagecoach*.

1. UJST
2. REHTE
3. AAWY
4. ORMF
5. HSTNIG
6. NAM
7. ELLW
8. ACN'T
9. RNU
10. EAR
11. MOES

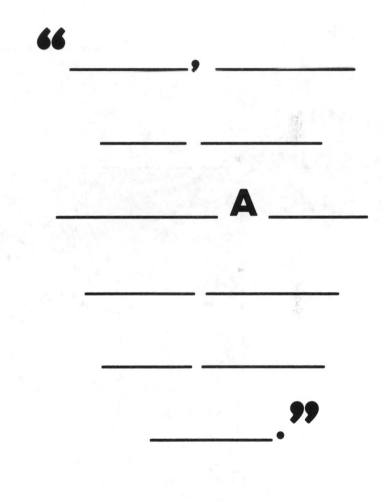

" _____, _____

____ ____

_____ A ____

____ ____

____ ____

_____. "

HINT:

This bit of wisdom comes from *Sands of Iwo Jima*.

1. LTEITL

2. ALFL

3. LFEI

4. NTOI

5. ARNI

6. STUM

7. HAEC

" __ __ __ __ __ __ __ __ __

__ __ __ A __ __ __ __ __

__ __ __ __ __ __

__ __ __ __ . "

Sands of Iwo Jima, 1949

HINT:

This romantic quote is from *Hondo*.

1. DNO'T
2. UGSES
3. TGO
4. PEOELP'S
5. HIWT
6. RHEATS
7. NTYGHANI
8. OD
9. NALCREDA
10. OT

Hondo, 1953

" I _____ _____

_____

_____ _____

_____ _____

___ _____ A

_____ . "

HINT:

Duke said this in an interview with *TIME* magazine in 1967.

1. HET

2. EVRE

3. SI

4. LLSE

5. OD

6. ADN

7. I'EV

8. RINSCIEYT

9. LELISGN

10. LAL

11. EENB

12. TUO

13. HLEL

14. TAHT

15. DRTTSAE

16. SICEN

17. FO

" ____ I ___ _

___ _____

___ ___ ____ _____

____ ___ ___ ___ _____

____ _____ I _____. "

The Big Trail,
1930

HINT: John Wayne's character said this in *The Big Trail*.

1. ALTRI

2. ARDPHISH

3. ON

4. IUTLB

5. EEVR

6. WSA

7. OUTHTWI

8. AREGT

" ___ _____ _____ ___

___ _____ _____

_____ . "

HINT:

This is how Quirt Evans feels about pancakes.

1. PPIEEATT
2. NDZEO
3. LEOS
4. FITSR
5. 'ME

6. ROF
7. ETH
8. AREFT
9. OLCEUP
10. YM

Angel and the Badman, 1947

"I _____

_____

_____ _____

_____ _____

_____

_____

_____ 'A

_____."

HINT: This quote is from *The Man Who Shot Liberty Valance*.

1. ENED

2. U'EYRO

3. FO

4. PIMRIGL

5. CESSTTHI

6. NOGNA

7. OPEUCL

" _____ ,

_____ _____

_____ A _____

____ _____ . "

The Man who Shot Liberty Valance, 1962

The Sons of Katie Elder, 1965

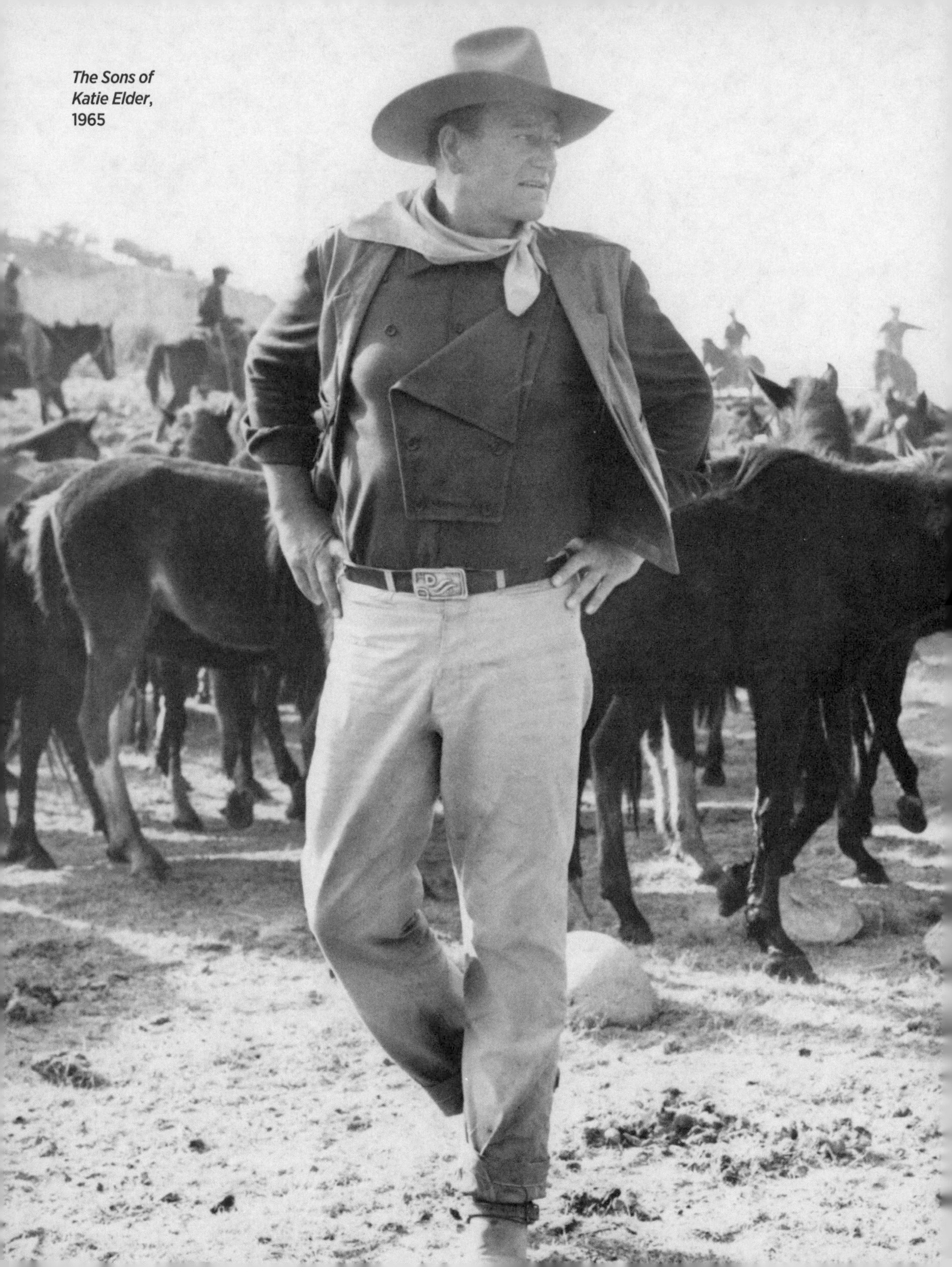

HINT:

Duke asked this in *The Sons of Katie Elder*.

1. SI
2. LNOOWDW
3. ETLL
4. SU
5. UOR

6. NCA
7. HTE
8. AP
9. TTHA
10. UYO

11. TRA
12. NKTSINI'
13. STOH
14. HWO
15. DYITR

" _____ _____ _____ _____

_____ _____ _____ _____

_____ _____

_____ _____ _____ ?"

HINT:

Duke's thoughts on the future.

1. **PMTITROAN**
2. **MOTS**
3. **FIEL**
4. **SI**
5. **OOMOTWRR**
6. **ITGHN**
7. **NI**
8. **HTE**

" _____ _____

__ ____ ____

_____

_____ __

____. "

Duke poses for the camera, 1975. He made two films that year: *Brannigan* and *Rooster Cogburn.*

HINT:

This quote is from *Donovan's Reef*.

1. STRSA
2. NADTS
3. BEVIHAOR
4. LLEW
5. DNO'T

6. OOGD
7. ROF
8. ETHOS
9. DGOL

" _____ , _____ _____

_____ _____ _____

_____ _____ _____ . "

Donovan's Reef, 1963

HINT:

This classic quote is from *She Wore a Yellow Ribbon.*

1. EVNRE

2. AESNSEKW

3. FO

4. NIGS

5. TI'S

6. PALIEGOOZ

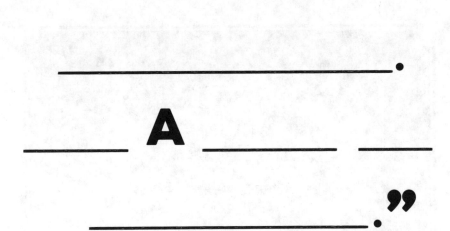

" _____

_____.

____ A _____ ___

_____.''

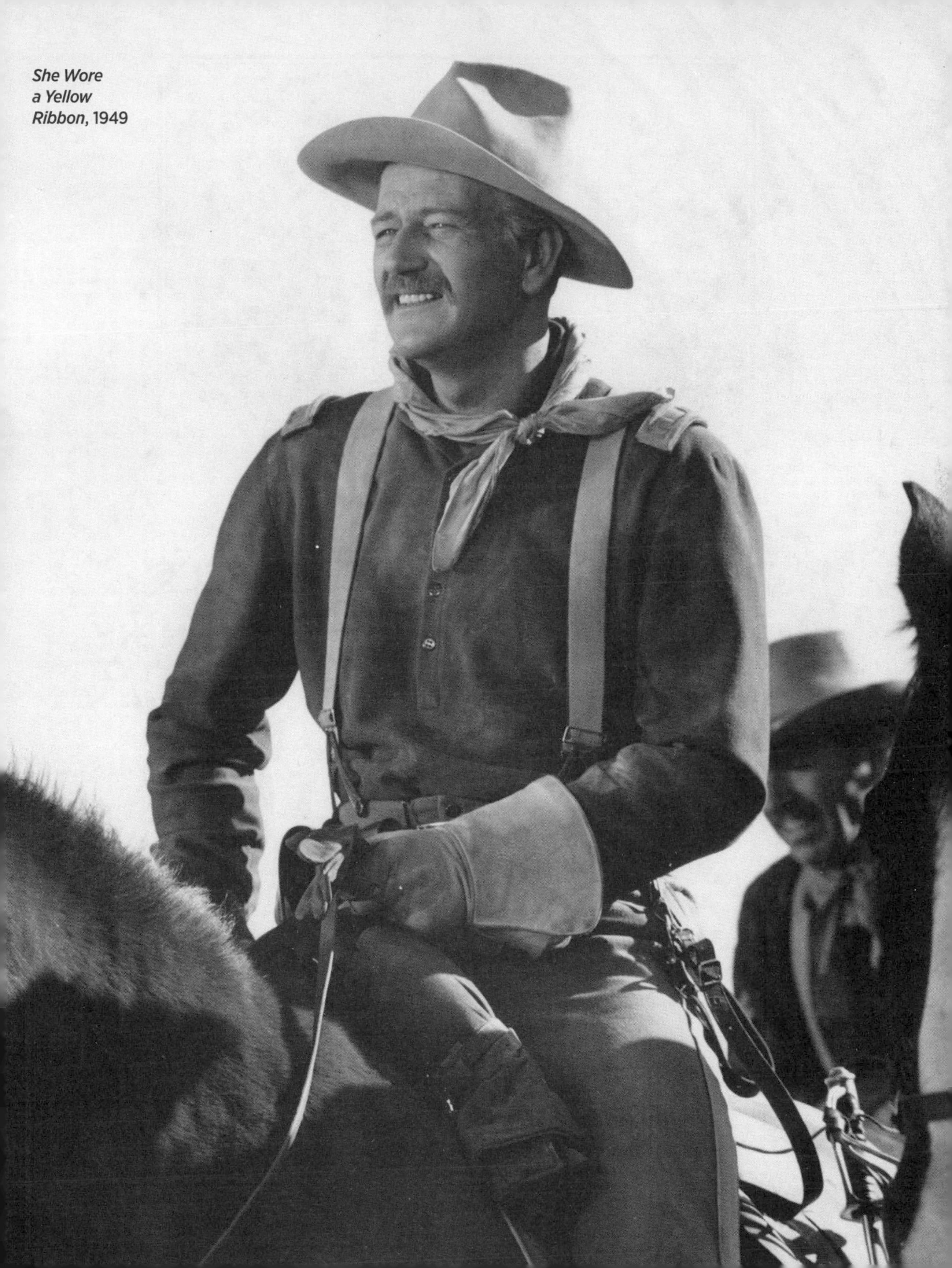

She Wore a Yellow Ribbon, 1949

The Shootist,
1976

HINT: Duke said this in his final film, *The Shootist*.

1. TI

2. NTSOUC

3. AHTT

4. GIENB

5. IGLNWIL

6. RO

7. EVNE

8. NSI'T

9. ALAWSY

10. TARCEAUC

11. TI'S

12. GNBIE

13. TFSA

HINT:

This quote is from *Big Jake*.

1. GLNO
2. UHOTM
3. NO
4. ADN
5. ASRE
6. OYU'RE
7. NO
8. HROTS

Big Jake, 1971

" _____ _____ _____

_____ _____ _____

_____ _____. "

Red River,
1948

HINT:

Duke says this in *Red River*.

1. TSIH
2. DWORL
3. TECNARI
4. IOTNHNG
5. EW

6. GBROUHT
7. RCARY
8. TI'S
9. UTO
10. EW

11. NAC
12. DNA
13. ITONGHN
14. IOTN

66 ___ _____

_____ _____ _____

_____ _____ _____

_____ _____ _____. 99

HINT: This quote is from *McLintock!*

1. UERBCUAATR
2. GHVAENRO
3. UPHS
4. FO
5. TOG

6. I'EV
7. EM
8. TOUHC
9. DNO'T

" _____ _____ A

_____ __

_____ ,

_____ .

_____ _____ _____ . "

McLintock!,
1963

HINT:

Duke said this one-liner in *El Dorado*.

1. AMN'S

2. ERTHE

3. OBY

4. TUO

5. OD

6. OT

7. YUO

8. FLTE

9. JBO

" ___ ___

A ___ ___

___ ___ ___ ___

A ___ ___ !"

El Dorado, 1967

HINT:

John Wayne lived by these words.

1. WOL

2. LATK

3. NOD'T

4. SYA

5. DNA

6. MCUH

7. WSLO

8. OTO

9. LTAK

Duke c. 1944, during his first decade of being a household name.

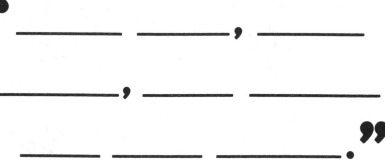

" _____ _____ , _____

_____ , _____ _____

_____ _____ _____ . "

Ride Him, Cowboy, 1932

HINT:

Duke said this in *Ride Him, Cowboy*.

1. EHSSRO
2. TAEM
3. OFRM
4. EW
5. 'ME

6. ETG
7. NDO'T
8. ENWH
9. YETH
10. SHTOO

11. WHREE
12. EW
13. MOEC
14. YRONER

'Neath the Arizona Skies, 1934

HINT: According to Duke in *'Neath the Arizona Skies*, some men are tougher read than others.

1. WEIRNTT 4. LKIE 7. EAR

2. NEM 5. ELANGUGA 8. STAGREN

3. NI 6. SEMO 9. SOBOK

" ____ ___ _ ___

____ _____ _A

_____ _____. "

HINT:

This favorite Duke quote is from *Rio Bravo*.

1. NDEO

2. NOD'T

3. OSRRY

4. DUED

5. EGT

6. TI

" _____ _____ ____

__ _____ , _____ . "

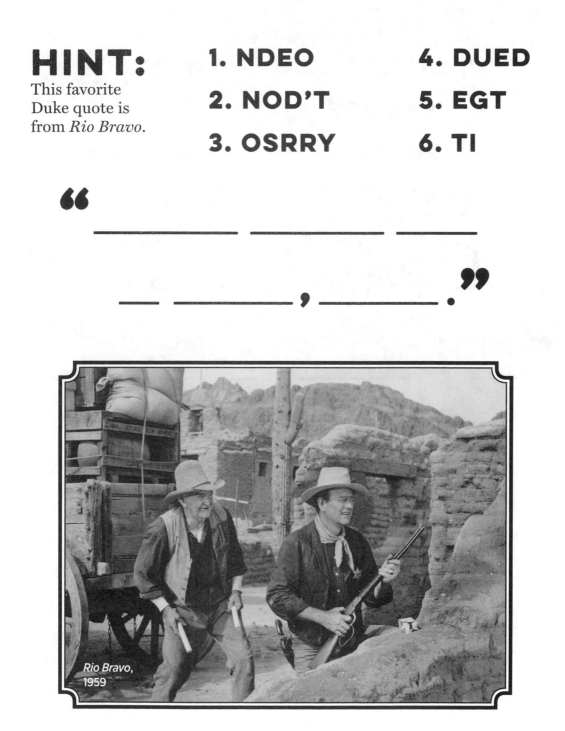

Rio Bravo,
1959

HINT:
John Wayne said this while accepting his Oscar for *True Grit*.

1. OUDLW
2. ILEARRE
3. PACTH
4. HATT
5. FI
6. AHVE

7. TPU
8. TTHA
9. WKONN
10. NO
11. RAYSE
12. DAH

" __ I _____ _____

_____ I _____

_____ ___ _ _____

_____ ___ **35**

_____ _____ . "

Barbra Streisand congratulates Duke on his Oscar, 1970.

HINT:

This zinger is from *Chisum*.

1. UTJS
2. NOD'T
3. RAVFO
4. LWLE
5. OT
6. NOEC
7. BTU
8. LI'L
9. KNTLAGI
10. OT
11. UOY
12. KTLA
13. ITSH
14. NEVRIM

" _____ I _____

_____ _____

___ _____ , ____

_____ _____ ___

_____ _____ ___ ___

_____ . "

Chisum, 1970

HINT:

This quote is from
Rio Lobo.

1. I'EV

2. EDLLAC

3. TLO

4. UBT

5. FO

6. ENEB

7. TON

8. HGNTSI

9. MBOFTROCEAL

Rio Lobo,
1970

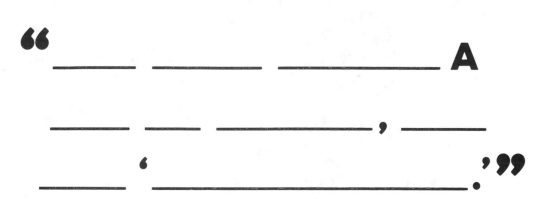

"_____ _____ _____ A
_____ __ _____, _____
'_____.'"

True Grit,
1969

HINT:

This quote is from *True Grit*.

1. AHVE
2. OT
3. YNOBOD
4. IDDN'T
5. VENRE
6. OHST

"I _____ _____

_____ I

_____ _____ ___."

Rooster Cogburn, 1975

HINT: Duke said this in *Rooster Cogburn.*

1. DAPYYA
2. YBOS
3. NDA
4. ETG

5. EOCM
6. TI
7. TI'S

"_____ _____,

_____, _____ _____

_____ __!"

HINT:

This insult comes from *Hellfighters*.

1. EFLOLW
2. RPBLAOBY
3. LUDCON'T
4. SA
5. IWTHOUT
6. EAR
7. OUY
8. YULG
9. TGE
10. OT
11. RIFTS
12. AEBS
13. SA
14. IFRE

Hellfighters,
1968

"A _____

_____ _____ ____

_____ __ ____

_____

_____

_____ ____ __

_____ ____ ___

_____A

____."

HINT:

This quote is from *She Wore a Yellow Ribbon*.

1. EBTARH
2. OGT
3. INCEM
4. NO
5. OYU

6. IPE
7. OTH
8. OUY
9. ELIK

" _____ _____

A _____

____ ____

____ A ____

_____ ___. "

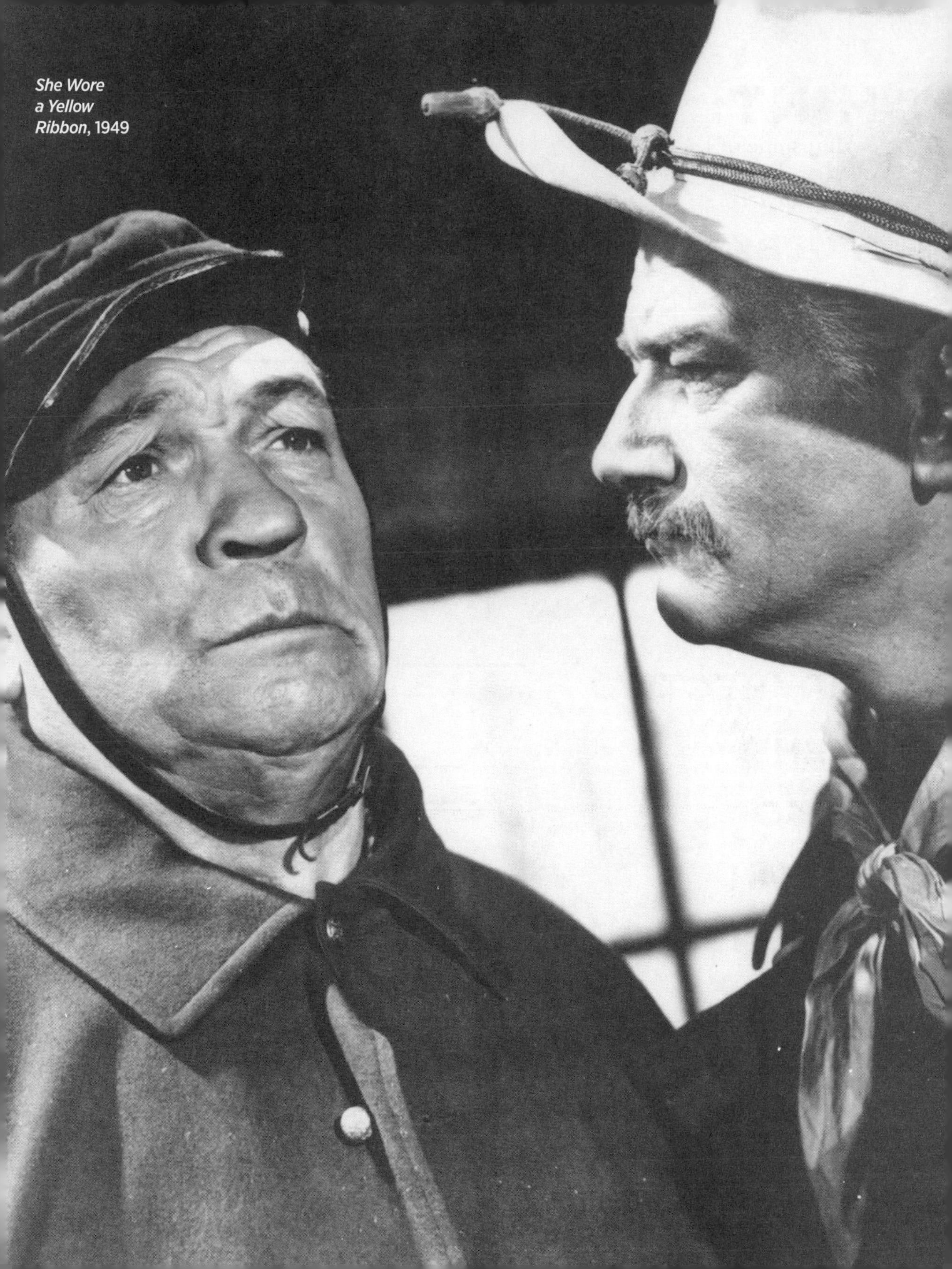

She Wore a Yellow Ribbon, 1949

HINT:

Perhaps one of Duke's best insults, this quote is from *Fort Apache*.

1. ULBKAGARCD
2. IRAL
3. TNOSEH
4. ADN
5. OYU'RE
6. TESNHC
7. NI
8. RYHECTPIO
9. EHT
10. FO
11. EMN
12. TSNORISL

" _____ A

_____ ,

A _____ , A

_____ ___

A _____ __

____ _____

___ _____ ___. "

Fort Apache,
1948

HINT:

This quote is from *Red River*.

1. IQEUTTSR

2. OUNEHG

3. OND'T

4. CEIPSAEYLL

5. WEHN

6. ETHY'ER

7. OTN

8. ISNHIF

9. TARST

10. OT

11. OOGD

12. HWAT

13. THYE

14. IKLE

Red River, 1948

"I _____ _____

_____,

_____ _____

_____ _____

_____ _____

__ __ _____ _____

_____ _____."

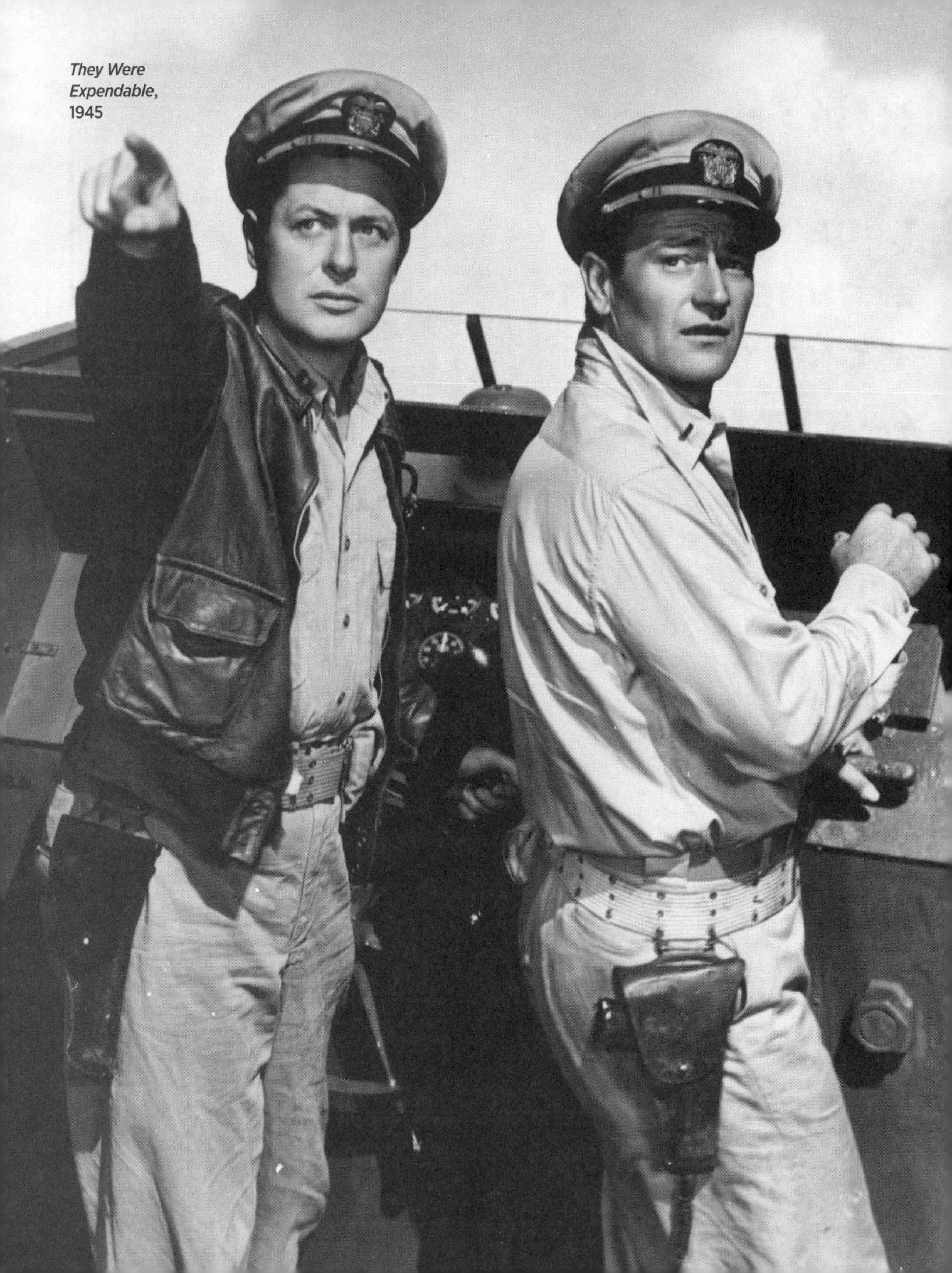

They Were Expendable, 1945

HINT:

This quote is from *They Were Expendable*.

1. RMOF
2. OWN
3. OEN
4. NO
5. NMA

6. 'MI
7. OS
8. BDAN
9. CLSTTIYR

" __ ____

____ __ __

_____ A ____

____ _____!"

HINT:

This quote is from *The Cowboys*.

1. EW'RE

2. OEMS

3. DLHYTAGI

4. NO

5. CBTSIIU

6. NAD

7. LASP

8. OG

9. ETL'S

10. AONBC

11. NNIURB'

The Cowboys, 1972

" _____ _____ _____

___ A _____ _____

_____ ___ ! _____

_____ _____ ! "

HINT:

This insult is from *'Neath the Arizona Skies*.

1. FO

2. KILE

3. OYU

4. SPIOON

5. IED

6. ENSAKS

7. HTREI

8. ONW

9. LAUUYSL

" _____ ____ ____

_____ ___ ___

_____ _____ _____."

'Neath the Arizona Skies, 1934

HINT:
This Duke quote is about bravery.

1. WODRS

2. MNAENGI

3. TSUJ

4. EFAR

5. FO

6. ETH

7. NYAM

8. NOE

9. ODN'T

10. OKWN

11. TEH

12. SI

13. FO

" _____ _____ _____

_____ _____ _____

_____ _____ I

_____ _____ _____ _____

_____ _____. "

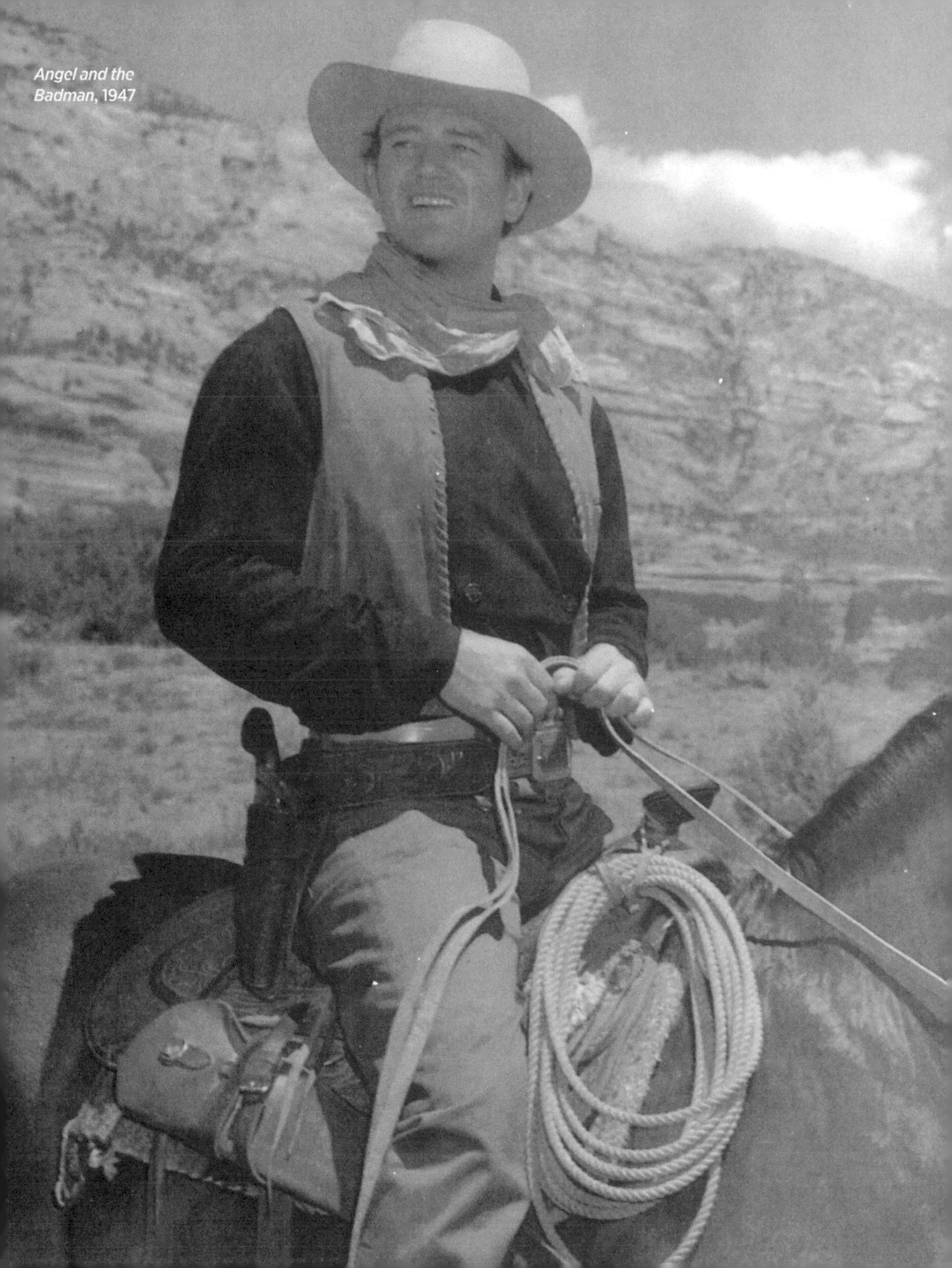

Angel and the Badman, 1947

HINT:

This quote is from *Stagecoach*.

"I _____ _____

_____ _____

_____ ___ _____

_____ ___

_____ ___ ___

_____ _____."

1. OSCEITY

2. UOY

3. ANC'T

4. SGUSE

5. TOU

6. FO

7. EKWE

8. ADN

9. NITO

10. ABREK

11. NI

12. EHT

13. SMAE

14. RINPSO

Stagecoach, 1939

HINT:

This classic quote is from *In Harm's Way*.

1. MSLOEPEAC

2. TBATLES

3. REA

4. REARTH

5. YB

6. LAL

7. NEM

8. CSEDRA

9. HOW'D

10. EB

11. GHFOUT

12. LESE

In Harm's Way, 1965

" _____ _____

_____ _____ ___

_____ ___

_____ ___

___ _____

_____ . "

El Dorado,
1967

HINT:

This quote is from *El Dorado*.

1. HYTE'ER
2. TIEM
3. OYU
4. 'ME
5. XNET

6. DNO'T
7. DEDA
8. ENAR
9. SEMOYDOB
10. 'ILT

11. OYU'ER
12. ESUR
13. OHOST
14. OG

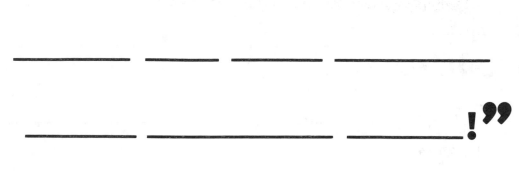

"_____ _____ _____ _____

_____, _____ _____

_____ _____ _____

_____ _____ _____!"

HINT:

Duke said this in *The Shootist*.

1. TBETER

2. UYO

3. ITOSPL

4. EGT

5. EIFNRD

6. NIEL

7. FO

8. ODN'T

9. ITHS

10. NOE

12. URES

13. ORKW

14. TFI

15. UYRO

16. NHTAEOR

The Shootist, 1976

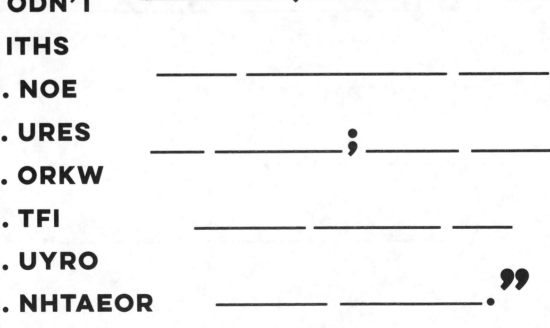

" _____, ____ ____

____ _____ ___ ____

__ _____; ___ ___

____ ____ ___ ____

_____ _____. "

1. RLEAN
2. OYU
3. ASFT
4. IGHTR
5. NAD
6. OYU
7. AOTTG
8. ALREN
9. OTGTA

" _____ _____ _____

_____ _____ _____

_____ _____ _____ . "

Sands of Iwo Jima, 1949

HINT:  This quote is from *Hondo*.

1. HOUTGA
2. TSBE
3. OD
4. WATH

5. EH
6. AMN
7. IS
8. HTISNK

"A _____

_____

___ _____

___ _____."

Hondo, 1953

HINT:

This quote is from *The Horse Soldiers*.

1. HTE

2. HMI

3. THTA

4. RAM

5. OKTO

6. FITGH

7. FO

8. SMOE

9. IOLSGN

10. UOT

11. FO

12. EBYAM

" _____ _____

_____ _____

_____ _____ _____

_____ _____

_____ _____ . "

The Horse Soldiers, 1959

The Man Who Shot Liberty Valance, 1962

HINT:

Duke said this line in *The Man Who Shot Liberty Valance.*

1. IGLPIRM

2. AKTE

3. HWAO

4. ASYE

5. HETER

6. 'RE

" _____ , _____ _____ _____

_____ , _____ . "

The Longest Day, 1962

HINT:

This quote is from *The Longest Day*.

1. HLEL
2. UYO
3. GVIE
4. TEH
5. NCA'T

6. BERAK
7. EDNS
8. IHM
9. OT
10. NEYEM

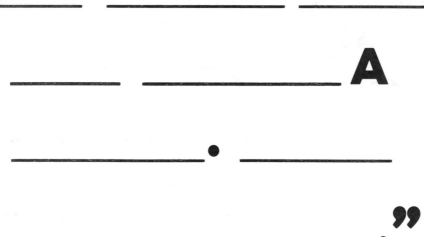

_____ _____ _____

_____ _____ **A**

_____ • _____

_____ _____ _____.

HINT:

This quote is from *She Wore a Yellow Ribbon.*

1. MRAY

2. ANSSOSE

3. ADN

4. HET

5. ONOM

6. SNU

7. BTU

8. HTE

9. EHNGAC

10. SNWOK

11. ON

12. HTE

She Wore a Yellow Ribbon, 1949

"_____ _____ _____ _____

_____ _____,

_____ _____ _____

_____ _____

_____."

HINT:

Duke says this in *The Alamo*.

1. RWGON
2. HRTEE'S
3. NDA
4. HET
5. OD
6. OYU
7. TGOAT
8. GRITH
9. NOE
10. RO
11. HSTERE'
12. THOER

" _____ _____ ___

_____ _____.

___ _____ _ ____.''

The Alamo, 1960

HINT: This declaration is from *The Shootist*.

1. AHND
2. EB
3. OWN'T
4. NWO'T
5. EB
6. NO
7. NDA
8. EGNRDOW
9. EB
10. ALID
11. OWN'T
12. SINTULDE

"I ________ ____

______________, I __________

___ ____________, ______

I ________ ___ ______ A

________ ____."

The Shootist,
1976

HINT:
This quote is from *Chisum*.

" _____ _____

1. **ENBIHGORS**   ____ ____ ____

2. **MYA**   ____ ____ ____I

3. **ODN'T**

4. **ENLIGHBORY**   ____ ____ ____

5. **EB**   __ _____."

6. **OT**

7. **TBU**

8. **OT**

9. **HEAV**

10. **VHAE**

11. **EB**

12. **EW**

Chisum, 1970

HINT:

Duke said this in *The Cowboys*.

1. ILLGACN

2. AMKE

3. ONS

4. TI

5. FO

6. UWOLDN'T

7. EM

8. TATH

9. HAIBT

The Cowboys, 1972

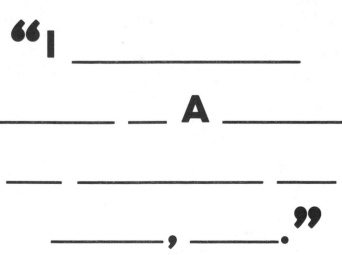

"I _____

_____ __ A _____

__ _____ __

_____, ___."

North to
Alaska,
1960

HINT: This quote shows just how much Duke loved America.

1. RFO
2. THWA
3. TTHA
4. EERYOENV
5. KONW
6. OVEL

7. ROU
8. SNTADS
9. FRO
10. PHOE
11. HES
12. APRYER

13. OCURNTY
14. WAHT
15. HSE
16. YM
17. RELLYA

"__ ___ AND _____ IS ___ _____ ___ AND

___ __ _____ ___

_____ __ _____ IS AND

___ __ _____ ___."

The Man Who Shot Liberty Valance, 1962

HINT: This quote is from *The Man Who Shot Liberty Valance*.

1. NKDRI

2. AMN

3. VAHE

4. ACN'T

5. EPACE

6. HTIS

7. OTWN

8. NI

9. AORNDU

" _____ A _____ _____ A

_____ _____ _____

_____ _ _____ ?"

HINT:

Duke said this in *Rio Grande*.

1. IUTDCNTRESO

2. EH

3. ANTYIHNG

4. TBU

5. HSI

6. AMN'S

7. LAERN

8. OT

9. RODW

10. NROOH

11. ISH

12. WNO

13. VEEN

14. SI

15. TATH

16. MUTS

Rio Grande, 1950

" _____ __ _____ _____

_____ A _____ _____ _____

_____, _____ __

__ _____, __

__ _____ . "

HINT:

This quote is from *The Sea Chase*.

1. USCCSES
2. FOCUNSE
3. RPPOSEU
4. FO

5. NDO'T
6. HWTI
7. ICENISTRY

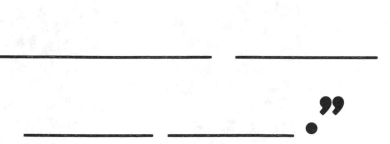

HINT:

This quote is from *The Comancheros.*

1. EMAN
2. RAE
3. YSA
4. ORDWS
5. AHWT
6. YB
7. RWOSD
8. YTHE
9. EMN
10. NAD
11. EILV

"
_____ _____

_____ _____

_____ •••

_____

_____ _____

_____ _____ •

The Comancheros, 1961

HINT:

Duke said this line in *Chisum*.

1. PELOPE

2. ON

3. EOORNS

4. EWHRE

5. EUBCASE

6. OG

7. TRAMET

8. RO

9. ALW

10. HRETE'S

11. HTE

12. ETRLA

Chisum, 1970

" _____ ____

_____ _____

_____ ___,

_____ ___

_____ _____

_____ _____ . "

HINT: This line is from *The Searchers*.

1. RAPNYIG

2. EAMN

3. HEETR'S

4. ITME

5. OFR

6. OMRE

7. ON

_____ ____

_____ ___ ____

_____! ____!"

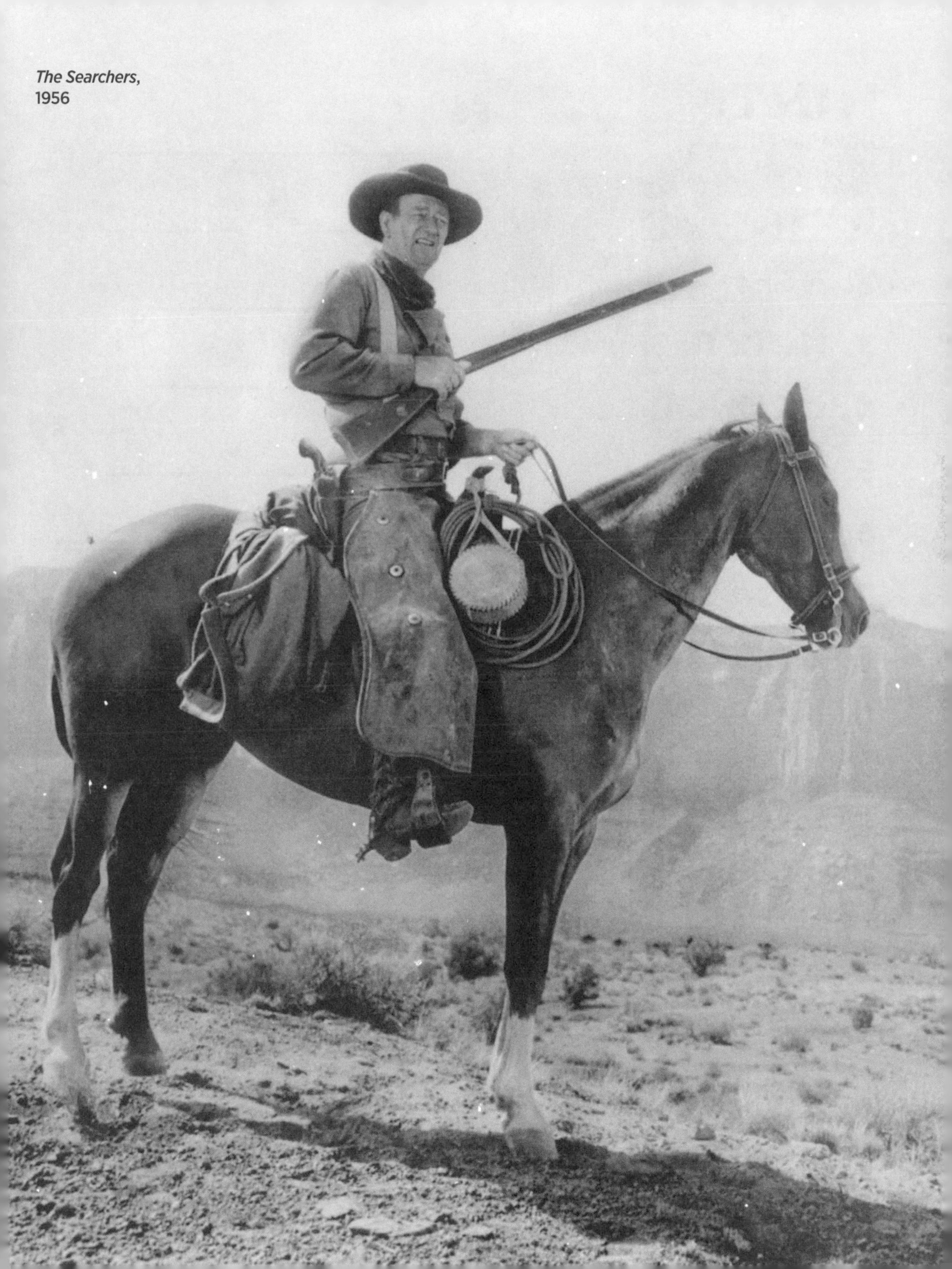

The Searchers,
1956

HINT:

Duke says this in *McLintock!*

1. YSA

2. NFEI

3. NOD'T

4. ORNNGIM

5. RO

6. LI'L

7. TI'S

8. OHOST

9. AY

" _____ _____ _ _____

_____ A _____ _____

_____ _____

_____ _ _____

_____ _____ _____."

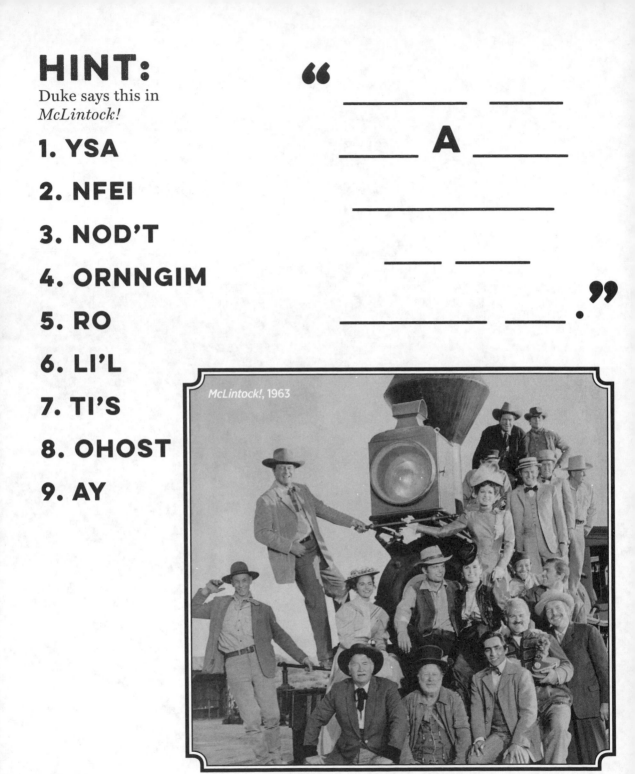

McLintock!, 1963

HINT:

This quote is Duke's description of himself.

1. OTEETISRNVDAM

2. MA

3. YBAB

4. ATTH'S

5. PPEUR

6. NMA

7. DAN

8. RPIEKC

9. ISKESR

10. YM

11. GRHEGU

12. TNURAE

John Wayne holding a young'un.

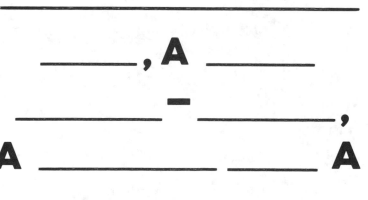

"I __ __ A

_____

_____ , A _____

_____ - _____ ,

A _____ _____ A

_____ - _____

_____ _____ . "

Cast a Giant Shadow, 1966

SPOT THE DIFFERENCE

See if you can find all the changes
made to the following John Wayne
movie stills and posters.

Can you find the five (5) changes made to this still from *Desert Trail* (1935)?

There are seven (7) differences between these two movie posters.

Spot the six (6) differences in this still from *Lawless Range* (1935).

See if you can find the seven (7) differences between these two posters.

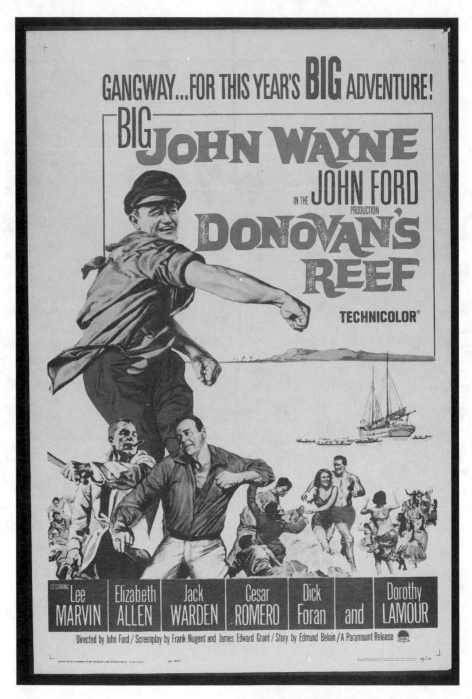

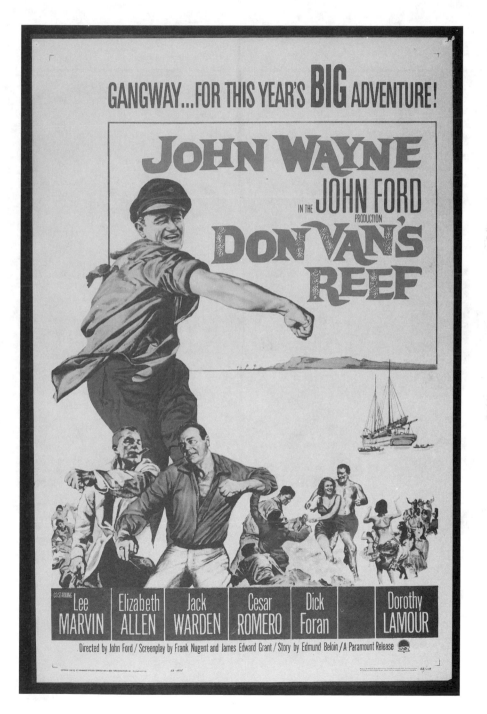

Can you spot the five (5) differences in this scene from *In Old Oklahoma* (1943)?

See if you can find the six (6) changes made to this poster.

Find the five (5) changes made to this scene from *Angel and the Badman* (1947).

There are five (5) differences between these two Duke posters.

Six (6) changes have been made to this scene from *Fort Apache* (1948).

See if you can spot the six (6) differences between these two posters.

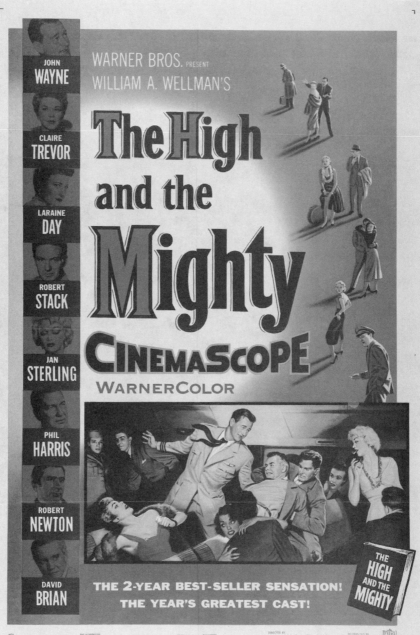

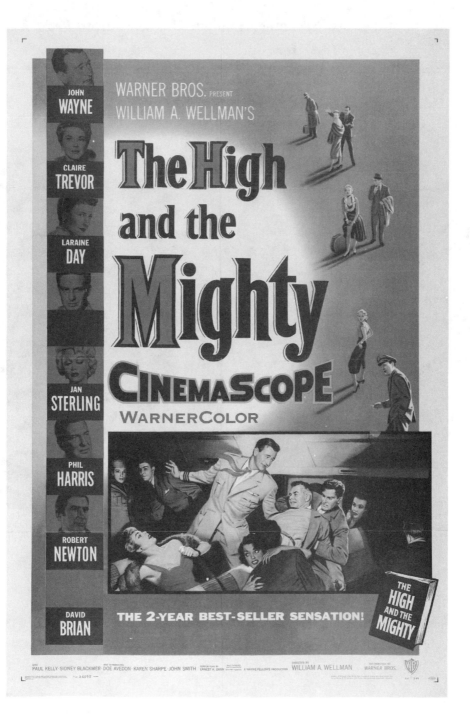

See if you can find all six (6) changes made to this scene from *Red River* (1948).

Six (6) changes have been made to this classic poster.

There are six (6) differences in this still from *The Fighting Kentuckian* (1949).

Spot the five (5) differences between these two posters.

There are five (5) differences in this scene from *Operation Pacific* (1951).

Can you find the six (6) changes that have been made to this poster?

See if you can spot the five (5) differences in this scene from *Jet Pilot* (1957).

See if you can spot the five (5) differences between these two posters.

Can you find the five (5) differences in this scene from *Rio Bravo* (1959)?

Can you find the five (5) changes made to this poster?

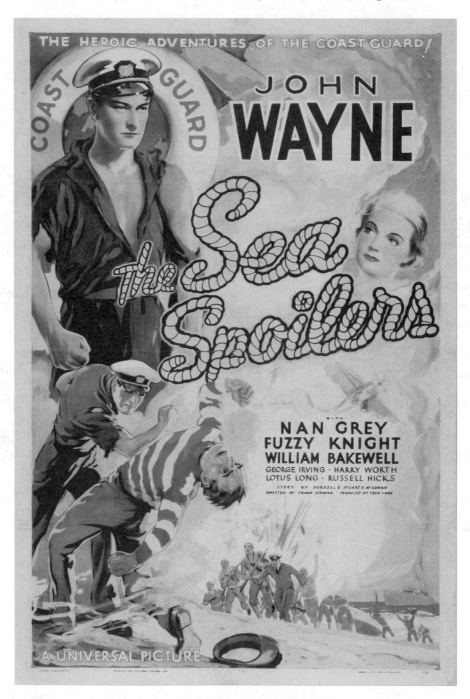

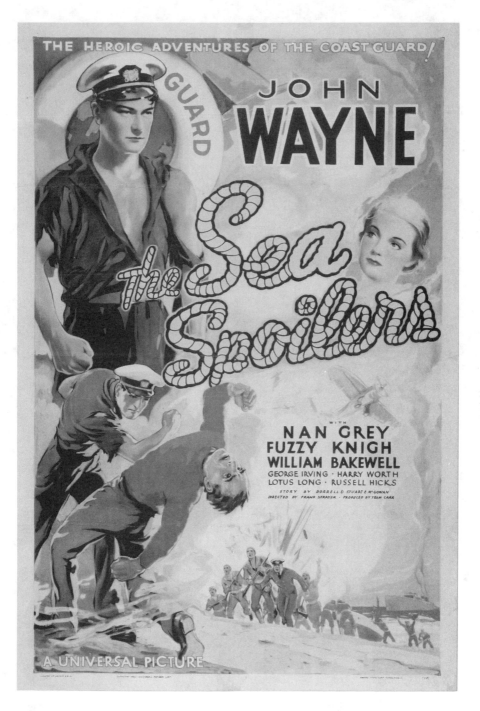

SU-DUKE-U

To solve Su-Duke-U puzzles, fill all the empty squares so that the numbers 1 through 9 appear once each in every column, row and 3x3 box.

☆ LEVEL OF DIFFICULTY ☆

Piece of Cake

Not So Simple

Head Scratching

Brain Breaking

		2				3	1	
				8	2		6	
		7	1	3	6	4		
					3	8		
3		9	8		7	5		4
		8	2					
		6	7	4	8	2		
	1		3	6				
	8	5				6		

7	9				4	2		
		4			6			7
2	6		9	3				8
	7			9	2			4
4	5						6	2
9			4	6			5	
5				4	8		7	1
8			6			3		
		3	2				4	9

1			3			2		9
3		7		5	4			
		2				7		
6				3	2			8
	8	3				1	2	
4			7	9				5
		6				4		
			4	7		6		1
7		4			1			2

2	7					1	3	6
	6	9		4		5	7	
							2	
		1		2	5			
4		5	7	1	6	2		3
			4	9		8		
	4							
	9	8		7		6	4	
6	1	2					8	9

	4		7			8		2
2		7	8		6		9	
3				9				
	9	2			8		4	
	3		5		4		2	
	6		9			1	7	
				1				3
	8		2		9	6		7
5		6			7		1	

7	3	6		9				
9			6			3		
	4		3				2	
	8	5		2		4		
1	6	4				8	7	2
		7		4		5	6	
	7				3		5	
		2			4			1
				8		7	9	4

		5			9		2	
9	3	7		1				
	1			8		3		9
	2	1			3			
	5	8	1		4	7	9	
			2			8	3	
6		3		4			8	
				3		9	1	4
	7		9			5		

					4	8		9
		6		2		7		1
	8	7			6		2	
2		8	4		3	1		6
				8				
7		1	6		2	4		3
	6		8			3	7	
4		9		3		6		
8		3	1					

4	5		1			6		
	9		6	5			4	3
		6		2			9	5
		4	5		8			
		3		4		5		
			3		2	9		
6	3			1		8		
2	8			3	6		1	
		9			5		7	6

6		3	2		4			5
	4			6	5	8		3
							7	
	2	6	9				3	
8	9			3			5	7
	5				7	9	8	
	1							
9		7	3	1			4	
2			5		6	7		9

		4	8		5	3		
	7	6		1				
		3			7	6	1	8
6	5			3			8	
9			1		4			3
	4			8			5	7
4	6	9	2			8		
				9		7	4	
		5	3		8	1		

4			5		1			
2	1	8				5	6	
		5	6	8	4		9	
		7		3	9	6		
	8						3	
		3	8	1		7		
	7		1	4	6	9		
	5	9				1	4	6
			9		8			7

1	2	5	6	4		7	3	8
					8	1		
						9	6	
			8	3	7	6	5	
		3				8		
	8	7	9	5	2			
	3	2						
		9	4					
7	4	6		1	5	3	8	9

	5	8	4				1	3
4						6		9
		6	2				5	8
9				7	5			
		2			3			
		5		9				2
3	6				5	9		
5		7						1
8	4				7	2	3	

5		2	9				7	4
6			2					9
		9				2	8	
			3		9	4	6	
9			8	4	1			2
	2	4	7		6			
	3	6				5		
4					8			6
2	9				4	1		8

2	8	3		7				
7	4			6				9
	1						8	
	3		6	9		8	5	
8								4
	9	2		4	3		6	
	5						4	
6				8			2	1
				1		9	7	3

		6		4	2		5	1
4	2					6	7	
8				1		4		
			7		5			6
		4		8		7		
1			9		4			
		8		9				7
	5	3					8	9
9	1		2	3		5		

		6		4				
9		1	5	2	8			
4	2						1	
7	5	3	2		4			8
	2		8		7	6		
6			1		9	2	5	7
	7						8	2
			9	8	5	7		1
				7		9		

	5	9			4	6		
7	8		2					4
					8	5	3	2
		6				3		9
9		2		5		8		1
5		4				2		
1	4	8	6					
6					2		8	3
		5	8			9	1	

8			2		3	4		1
		5	8			6		2
2							3	
		6	5				4	3
4		8				9		6
3	7				6	2		
	9							7
7		2			1	5		
5		3	6		7			8

4	5	2			1	9	3	8
	9	1	5			7		
						6		
				2		8	7	
1			9		4			3
	4	6		5				
		4						
		9			5	2	1	
2	7	8	6			4	9	5

	8		7	6	1	2		
	1	5			4	9		
	3			9	5			
	6		1	3				
	4	9				6	3	
				5	6		7	
			6	1			8	
		1	5			3	9	
		6	9	8	3		4	

	3					6		5
5	1		2				4	
9					5		2	8
		9	5		6		8	
3	4			2			7	1
	8		1		4	9		
2	5		6					7
	9				1		5	4
4		1					3	

	5			4	1			
7			9			2	1	4
			7				5	6
4			1					
	9			6			4	
					8			9
8	1				4			
9	2	6			7			1
			6	1			9	

5					2			
2	9		6			5	8	
	6	3	4					
3							1	
8			1		9	7			6
	7							9
					8	1	4	
		2	9		4		7	8
			6					2

	3	9			4		7	1
4								
6		7		8		4	9	
		6		4	1			
3			9		5			4
			3	7		2		
	5	3		9		1		8
								9
1	9		5			6	4	

			1					
		1	6	2			7	
	7	9				2		1
2			4				3	5
	1			7			9	
3	4				8			2
7		2				4	1	
	8			4	9	3		
					2			

6			9		2			
	2		5	7				3
1			3			8		
4		9					3	
		3		2		5		
	7					9		1
		2			4			6
3				9	1		7	
			6		5			8

		7			8			
	8			3				2
	3		4		9	6	5	
				9		4	7	3
7	5	9		4				
	7	8	3		1		6	
6				8			1	
			7			5		

		1	5	8		3	2	
						9		
2	8		4					1
3				7		4		
6		4		5		1		7
		5		4				9
9					4		1	3
		7						
	2	6		1	3	7		

6	2	3	9	4				
	9					2		
			3				4	
9		1		6			2	3
	2			9		7		
4	3			7		5		1
	4				7			
	7						5	
				3	8	9	7	6

	4	8		1		6		
		2	8	4		9		
								5
7	6				2			8
	9		6		7		5	
2			3				6	4
5								
		1		3	8	5		
		9		7		3	4	

					8	7	9	
			7	2	9			5
9				1			6	
	2	8		9			3	
			4		1			
	6			3		5	4	
	9			8				6
2			1	6	3			
	8	3	9					

5	9				2			8
		4	3				9	
					9	1	6	4
	5		6	1				
6			7		8			1
			2	3			8	
4	8	9	2					
	2				7	6		
1			9				2	3

4		7		1			3	
	6	5			3	8		
9				2				1
						4	6	
			7		8			
	9	4						
7				8				6
		9	6			5	8	
	4			5		1		3

	7				6			
	5						6	2
6	2	4			1			9
5		6		8	2			7
	4						9	
7			3	4		5		6
8			9			6	7	1
4	1						8	
			7				4	

3		8		6				9
		4	1		9		7	8
		7	5			6		
		2				9		4
4		5				3		
		3			8	5		
8	5		3		6	7		
2				1		8		3

6			4					1
			3		2	8		
9	8	7	6		5		2	
5		3					8	
		8				1		
	4					6		3
	1		7		8	9	3	2
		6	9		4			
8					1			6

3	1	4					9	8
					4			2
					6	7		
				8		4		3
4			9	6	1			7
7		2		4				
		1	6					
9			2					
8	6					9	2	5

6		4	3					5
							3	4
9		5				2	7	
	6	8	1					
		9		5				
				3	4	8		
	9	1				5		3
5	7							
2					4	7		9

	1	6	4	5				
					6			
	5			1		4	8	
			2			3		4
	3			8			6	
9		4			3			
	9	8		4			7	
			9					
				7	5	2	4	

	6			1		7	4	
			7	9	5			
	8	9						
6		1	5					
	9						8	
					4	2		7
						1	2	
			2	5	3			
	5	4		7			3	

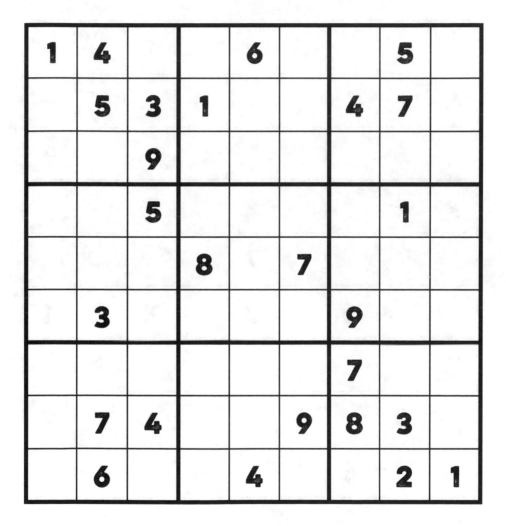

			5			1		
4				1	3		7	
	5							8
9	4	1		2		7		
				7				
		6		3		8	2	1
8							9	
	9		8	5				2
		4			6			

		1		8		4		
3				7		1		8
6			2				3	
							5	7
			3		4			
5	9							
	6				9			1
8		9		2				3
		5		4		8		

			7			9		8
					6			
				4		7	5	6
	6						1		7
		8	4	9	7	5		
3		7					9	
9	2	3		6				
			9					
6		4			8			

		2		6	7		9	8
	9			2		7	5	
						3		
						5	8	
		9				4		
	7	6						
		3						
	2	7		8			3	
6	1		7	9		2		

9				4				
				6	1			3
	5	3						6
		2			7	4		
	4	7		3		5	6	
		8	6			3		
2						7	1	
3			1	7				
				2				9

		9		1				7
5	4		3					8
					2			
			2	4			8	
1	7			8			4	9
	5			9	1			
			8					
9					7		1	3
3				2		8		

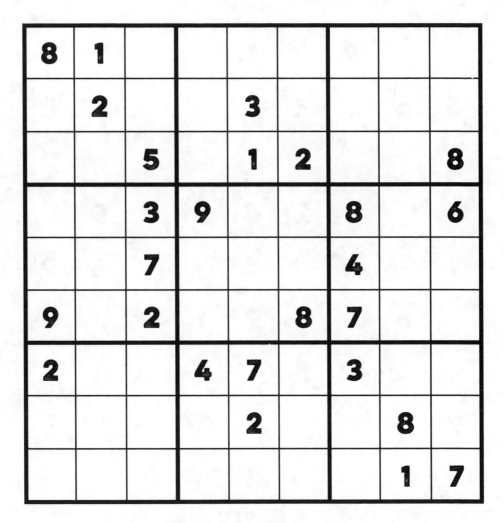

					8			6
		7		2				
9	1	4				3		
		6		9	3	5	1	
				5				
	3	5	2	7		8		
		8				7	4	1
				8		9		
1			5					

	2	9	5		6			
8	5						4	
		3						8
				6	1		7	
		1				6		
	8		3	5				
9						1		
	4						9	2
			2		9	3	6	

	2				7	1		
				8		5		3
			6	5				
		9			2		4	5
	7						6	
2	4		9			3		
				3	6			
8		1		2				
		3	8				2	

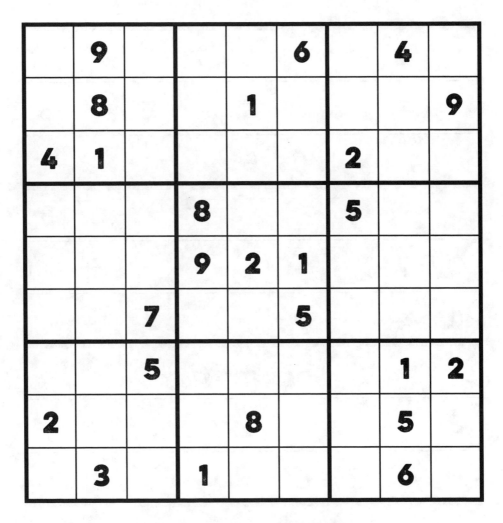

	9				6		4	
	8			1				9
4	1					2		
			8			5		
			9	2	1			
		7			5			
		5					1	2
2				8			5	
	3		1				6	

			2					
	2	1				5		8
	7		5					6
					4		3	
9		6				4		7
	5		3					
5					9		7	
3		8				2	6	
					6			

					7	1		
6				1	2		9	
9							6	
			9	2		7		4
	4						5	
8		3		5	4			
	3							5
	8		2	7				9
		2	4					

		5	7				6	
	6			4		2		
9	4	2						
7			6		4	8		
		9	8		5			7
						4	8	1
		4		1			2	
	2				6	7		

	6			3		2	7	
			4	1			3	
						6		
7	7	5			3		2	
			2		1			
1	1		9			3	4	
		6						
	2			8	5			
	5	3		2			1	

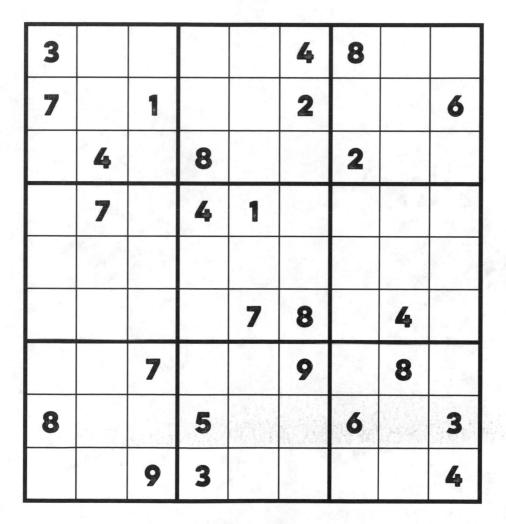

John Wayne
boosts morale in
Vietnam.

CLASSIC CROSSWORDS

See how much you remember about a few of Duke's best films, his personal life and some good ol' fashioned American history with these puzzles that are as timeless as John Wayne himself.

ALL ABOUT DUKE

Are you a true John Wayne fan? Test your knowledge with this classic Duke trivia crossword!

ACROSS

1. JW's second-oldest son

4. Duke and Ward Bond made a great one of these

6. *Donnybrook*! is a musical based on which JW film?

8. Ancient home of democracy

10. Home of Wayne's cattle: 26 _____ _____

13. 1980 Award, Congressional _____ Medal

14. 1970's Academy Award-winning character

16. Duke earned a _____ scholarship

18. Duke's first Best Actor-nominated film

20. JW's 1930 big break

22. "Out here, _____ is a bullet."

24. John Wayne _____ Foundation

25. JW's given first name

DOWN

2. First film produced by JW

3. Ringo Kid flick

5. Director Hawks and Duke's river

6. Duke's final film

7. The Morrisons traveled to California from _____ (long distance)

8. Attended _____ High School

9. John Wayne Airport's state

11. Patrick Wayne's first film

12. JW's Boat

15. "You know, _____ isn't for me."

17. Common article found in JW movie titles

19. Costar George _____

21. *Fort Apache* costar Henry

22. The Morrison family's Airedale terrier

23. Leading lady O'Hara

26. John Wayne was born in this state

The Shootist, 1976

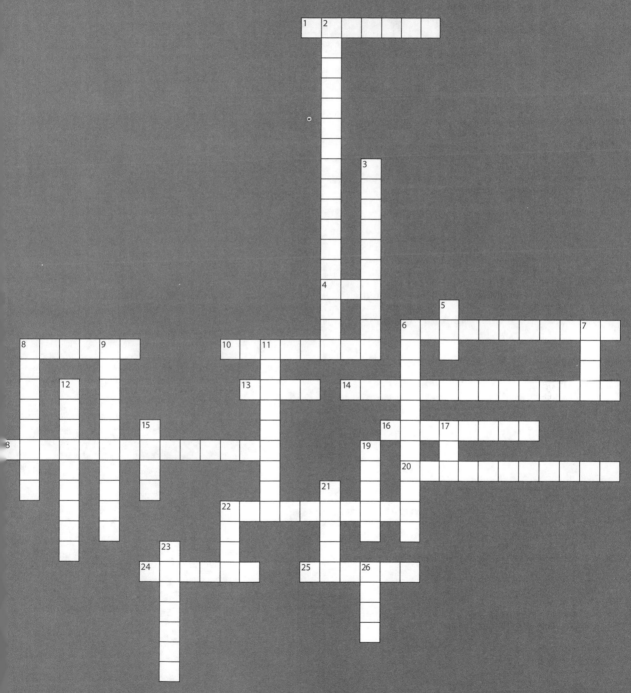

McLINTOCK!

See how much you know about this classic Western.

ACROSS

1. Coal shovel's alternate use

3. "Love in the _____," by The Limeliters

6. Duke's son and costar

7. One of Dev's skills

8. Sound a gun makes

11. "Any woman that allows a man to kiss her before they're formally engaged is a _____."

12. Refreshed noise after a glass of whiskey

13. Made more than $14 million at the ____ _____

16. Directed by Andrew _____

17. Made by _____ Productions

18. Junior, played by _____ Van Dyke

20. Estranged wife

21. G.W.'s daughter

DOWN

1. Loosely based on this playwright's work

2. Date of Comanche's breakout from jail

4. Movies require actors to film several of these

5. First movie fully produced by _____ Wayne

9. _____ Washington McLintock

10. "I've got a touch of _____, bureaucrat."

11. Released in Nineteen Sixty-_____

14. Stubborn partner will often put this down

15. Chief Puma of the _____ Tribe

16. Site of big, messy brawl

19. Junior's instrument of choice

McLintock! 1963

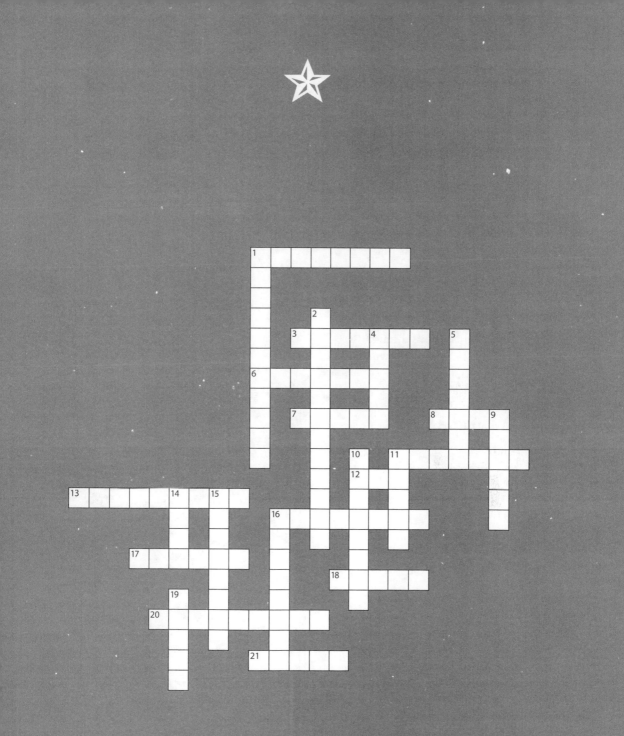

THE OLD WEST

Duke made dozens of Westerns—hopefully you learned a thing or two!

ACROSS

4. Doc Holliday's common-law wife

6. The _____ Purchase was made in 1803

10. Mail delivery system

13. Gunslingers stay _____ under pressure

14. He hunted and killed more than 4,000 Buffalo and later became a showman

16. Not a little, but a ____

17. Lonely drifter's favorite number

18. Brother of Wyatt Earp

19. Aces and eights

20. Folk hero "Wild Bill" _____

22. Infamous friend of Butch Cassidy

DOWN

1. Old West food truck

2. Famed war leader of the Lakota Sioux

3. The Wild West was the land west of the _____ River

5. Not a breakfast beverage for a real cowboy

7. Famous gunfight locale

8. Outlaw William H. Bonney's more famous nickname

9. Iconic hat

11. AKA Colt 45

12. The last president during the Wild West (1893–97)

15. Uncharted territory

21. Most famous member of the James-Younger Gang

22. Native American chief during the Wild West era

23. She shot to fame after besting marksman Frank E. Butler

Hondo, 1953

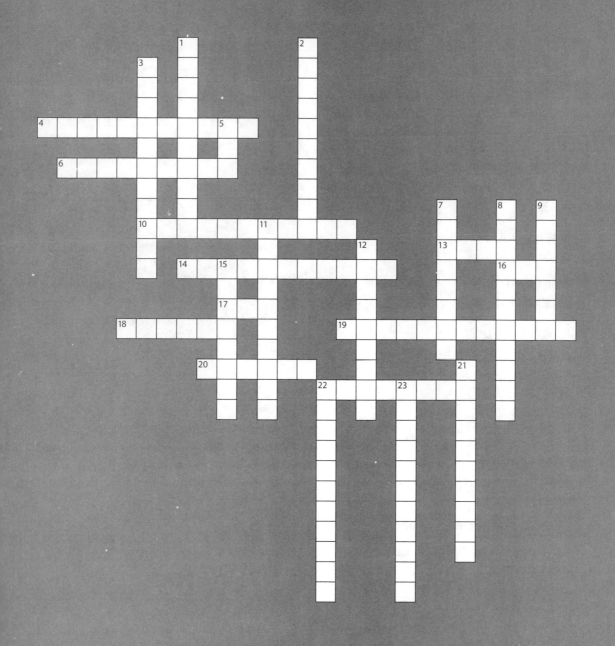

TRUE GRIT

The film for which Duke finally won an Academy Award.

ACROSS

5. The critter that almost kills Mattie

7. Chaney doesn't have a _____ what he's in for

8. Directed by Henry _____

9. La Boeuf's home state

10. Dennis Hopper

13. Mattie's Colt

14. Where Mattie finds Chaney

15. Won't shed one of these at film's end

17. Rooster often acts like this braying animal

18. Locale where Chaney is to be hanged

19. It's a _____ that Rooster gets his man

20. Mattie gets the money to pay Rooster by trading these

21. "I call that bold talk for a one-eyed ____ ____."

DOWN

1. "They tell me you're a man with _____ _____."

2. Title song performed by Glen _____

3. Released in Nineteen Sixty-_____

4. Rooster's profession

5. Rooster's given first name

6. Kim _____ as Mattie Ross

11. 1975 sequel

12. Based on the novel by Charles _____

13. "Lucky" Ned Pepper, actor

16. Lawyer J. Noble _____

True Grit, 1969

SUPPORTING THE TROOPS

Duke had the greatest respect for the Armed Forces, and he portrayed a member of every branch of the military in the course of his career.

ACROSS

2. Highest ranking officer in the Navy

5. 1936 JW Coast Guard flick

9. Basic training

10. The last military branch, founded in 1947

11. War fought during *The Green Berets* (1968)

14. Patriotic pastry

16. Axis power emblem (not setting)

17. Rebel general

18. Someone who is not in the Armed Forces

19. Military branch fighting in *Sands of Iwo Jima* (1949)

21. The only military organization assigned to the Department of Homeland Security

23. Bring a compass to find your ___

24. Lowest Army rank

DOWN

1. Oldest military award still given to U.S. military members

2. Absent without leave

3. *Flying _____*, 1951 Marine film

4. JW stars opposite Janet Leigh as an Air Force colonel in this movie

6. *Back to Bataan* (1945) takes place on the island of Luzon in the _____

7. WWII D-Day invasion locale

8. America's enemy in *They Were Expendable* (1945)

12. 1962 JW film about D-Day

13. JW's last black-and-white WWII epic

15. Alpha, Bravo, Charlie, _____, Echo

16. Duke becomes the commander of this kind of vessel in *Operation Pacific* (1951)

20. The Marine Corps is part of the _____

22. The Army's motto, This We'll _____

Duke visits the troops.

STAGECOACH

How well do you know Duke's breakout film?

Stagecoach,
1939

ACROSS

1. The stage driver's name

6. Where JW invites Dallas

8. Doc _____, played by Thomas Mitchell

9. Marion is Duke's real first _____

14. Doc served in the War of the _____

15. Doc suffers from _____

16. Mrs. Mallory delivers a baby _____

18. Group of cavalry soldiers

19. The Southern gentleman who is mortally wounded in the Apache attack

20. Marshal _____ Wilcox

22. Whiskey salesman Samuel _____

DOWN

2. Lead actress _____ Trevor

3. Apache leader _____

4. The stage's destination

5. Director's older brother/Billy the innkeeper

7. JW's character

10. Valley where the film was shot

11. Stuntman Yakima _____

12. Director

13. Released in Nineteen Thirty-_____

14. The U.S. Library of Congress selected *Stagecoach* for preservation in its National Film _____

17. The family that Duke is seeking vengeance against

19. Hatfield and Baker stop or _____ the stagecoach

21. Luke Plummer's hand is _____ and eights

RED RIVER

Duke's career took another leap forward when he
starred in this critically acclaimed box office hit.

ACROSS

1. Dunson needed money after
   the _____ War

3. This film made more than $9 million at
   the ____ office

8. Dunson decides to sell his herd in
   Sedalia, _____

9. Matt reroutes the herd toward the railroad
   in Abilene, _____

12. _____ breaks up the fight between
    Dunson and Matt

14. Dunson sets up his ranch in _____

15. Professional gunman Cherry _____

17. A good story

18. Trailhand Nadine _____,
    played by Walter Brennan

20. Footage from this film is in the opening
    montage of The _____ (1976)

21. "There are only two things more beautiful
    than a good gun: A Swiss watch or a
    woman from _____."

22. A _____ wagon is destroyed
    by a stampede

24. Tells the story of the first _____ drive

DOWN

2. Dunson's love interest is killed in an
   _____ attack

3. Based on the story "_____ Guns on the
   Chisholm Trail," by Borden Chase

4. Director Howard _____

5. Dunson's late mother's possession

6. Matt's love interest, Tess _____

7. Matthew Garth, played by _____
   Clift

10. "We brought nothing into this world and
    it's certain we can _____ nothing out."

11. Walter Brennan is also the
    film's _____

12. Goodbye

13. Dunson travels NE, not ___

16. Released in Nineteen Forty-_____

17. JW's character, _____ Dunson

19. Takes place along the _____ Trail

23. After winning a set of false teeth, his name
    is now "Two ____ Quo"

Red River,
1948

PATRIOTISM

"America is the land of freedom and that's the way I enjoy living."

ACROSS

6. The Civil War, Jazz Age and New Deal era are all different _____ in U.S. history

8. The _____ Twenties were followed by the Great Depression

9. JW's spoken word album, "America, _____"

10. First English settlement in the New World

15. Unalienable rights: Life, Liberty and the Pursuit of _____

17. "Sure I wave the _____ flag. Do you know a better flag to wave?"

21. Mt. _____ ; highest point in the U.S.

23. "O beautiful for _____ skies

24. The Declaration of Independence was signed in Seventeen-Seventy _____

25. This Duke film is all about ranch life in the American Old West!

DOWN

1. U.S. state west of Alabama

2. Author of the Declaration of Independence

3. The 4th POTUS

4. "Give me liberty or give me _____!" —Patrick Henry

5. Number of stripes on the US flag

7. The Star-Spangled Banner, by _____ Scott Key

11. The last state to join the Union

12. The Second Amendment gives individuals the right to _____

13. In 1980, JW was awarded the Presidential Medal of _____

14. In 1979, Duke was awarded a _____ Gold Medal

16. The country from which the Louisiana Purchase was made

18. Leader of the Continental Army

19. Wayne wrote to President _____ regarding the Panama Canal Treaty

20. The _____ Mountains are the longest mountain chain in the U.S.

22. "I didn't vote for him [_____] but he's my president, and I hope he does a good job."

26. In the Old West, people traveled by horse-_____ wagons

Sands of Iwo Jima, 1949

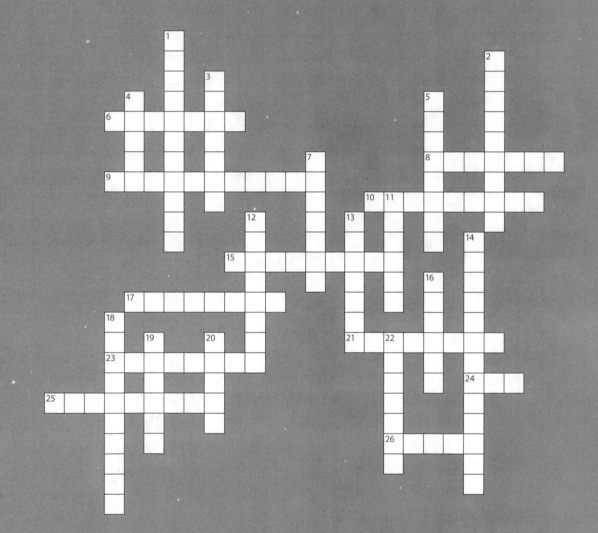

THE SHOOTIST

Test your knowledge of Duke's final film.

ACROSS

4. Richard _____ as Mike Sweeney

5. Gillom shoots the bartender before he can _____ his gun

6. Books is dying from _____

7. "I won't be wronged, I won't be _____ and I won't be laid a hand on."

11. Director Don _____

12. Two strangers tried to ambush Books while he slept, but he noticed their _____

16. Shoots Books in the back

17. Rogers's son Gillom, played by Ron _____

19. The film's original language

20. Duke wears a bolo style _____ in this film

21. Books's old flame

22. Paul Newman and Clint _____ passed on the roll before it was offered to Duke

DOWN

1. Books arrives in _____ City, Nevada

2. Released in Nineteen _____-Six

3. Bond Rogers, played by Lauren _____

4. Bond Rogers owns a _____ house

8. According to Books, being _____ counts more than being fast or accurate

9. Takes place in _____ Oh-One

10. J.B. or John _____ Books

11. Doc Hostetler, played by Jimmy _____

13. Based on the novel by Glendon _____

14. "Woman, I still have some _____."

15. Number of men Books asks to meet him on his birthday

18. "I don't believe I ever killed a man that didn't _____ it."

The Shootist, 1976

THE SEARCHERS

How well do you know this famous Duke Western?

ACROSS

3. What Ethan does to Scar, Debbie's kidnapper

6. What does Ethan Edwards absolutely not believe in?

9. "Let's go home, ____."

12. "That'll be the ____."

15. Ethan returns from the war with a _____ amount of gold

16. "Don't you think _____'s a chance we still might find her?"

18. Ethan nearly kills Debbie because of his hatred for ____ _____

19. The director of *The Searchers*

20. After Brad's death Ethan and Martin travel as a ____

21. "Figure a man's only good for one oath at a time; I took mine to the _____ States of America."

23. The Native American tribe that captured Ethan's niece

24. Amount of time Debbie is missing

25. Considered one of JW's best films of this genre

DOWN

1. The war that Ethan Edwards fought in

2. Laurie almost marries a man _____ Charlie McCorry in Martin's absence

4. This film also featured Duke's son ____

5. Name of Lucy's fiance

7. Martin's love interest

8. *The Searchers* is based on this woman's true story

10. Number of years Ethan Edwards was away

11. The name of Duke's character

13. Duke's costar, close friend and frequent collaborator

14. "I hope you die!" —_____

17. Another name for time period, such as Civil War_____

22. The Comanches believe they cannot enter the spirit-land without their ____

The Searchers, 1956

FINISH THE LIST

These puzzles are for ultimate John Wayne fans—see if you can complete each list without peeking at the answers!

MOVIES WITH MAUREEN

Duke made five movies with Maureen O'Hara as his costar. Can you name them all?

1. _____ **(1950)**

2. _____ **(1952)**

3. _____ **(1957)**

4. _____ **(1963)**

5. _____ **(1971)**

FAMILY MAN

John Wayne was the proud father of seven children. Do you know all their names?

1. _____

2. _____

3. _____

4. _____

5. _____

6. _____

7. _____

Duke with two of his
children, c. 1941.

Duke accepts his Oscar in 1970.

ACADEMY AWARDS

John Wayne was nominated for an Oscar three times
during the course of his career: twice for Best Actor and
once for Best Picture as a producer. Can you name the
films for which he was nominated?

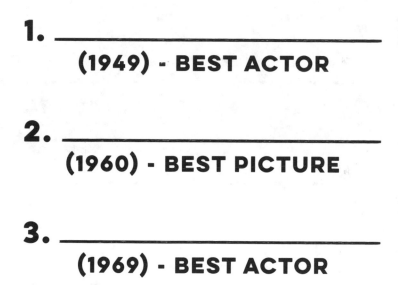

1. _____

(1949) - BEST ACTOR

2. _____

(1960) - BEST PICTURE

3. _____

(1969) - BEST ACTOR

THE FINAL TEN

In his last decade of filmmaking, Duke made 10 movies.
Starting with movies made in 1970, can you name them all?

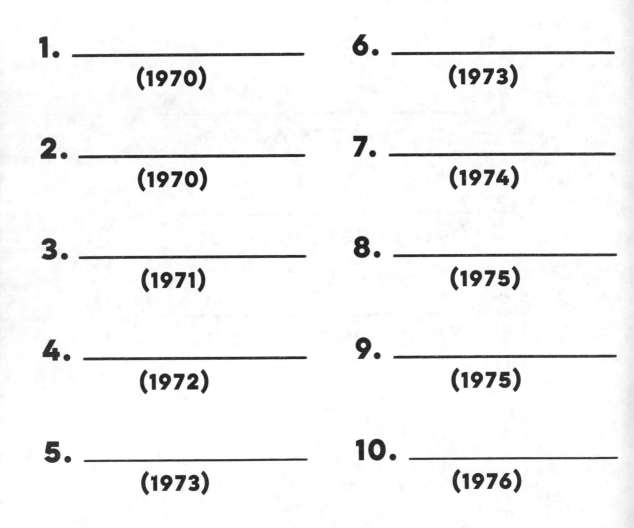

1. _____
(1970)

2. _____
(1970)

3. _____
(1971)

4. _____
(1972)

5. _____
(1973)

6. _____
(1973)

7. _____
(1974)

8. _____
(1975)

9. _____
(1975)

10. _____
(1976)

One of Duke's final films, 1974.

This cavalry
movie was
made in 1948

MILITARY MAN

John Wayne has represented every branch of the U.S. Armed Forces in his films—can you name each branch of the military?

1. _____

2. _____

3. _____

4. _____

5. _____

BONUS Duke also starred in John Ford's cavalry trilogy—can you name all three films?

1. _____ **2.** _____ **3.** _____

9 STRANGE PEOPLE

Stagecoach (1939) was the film that launched Duke to stardom and was "A Powerful Story of 9 Strange People." Can you name the nine characters the film focuses on?

1. _____

2. _____

3. _____

4. _____

5. _____

6. _____

7. _____

8. _____

9. _____

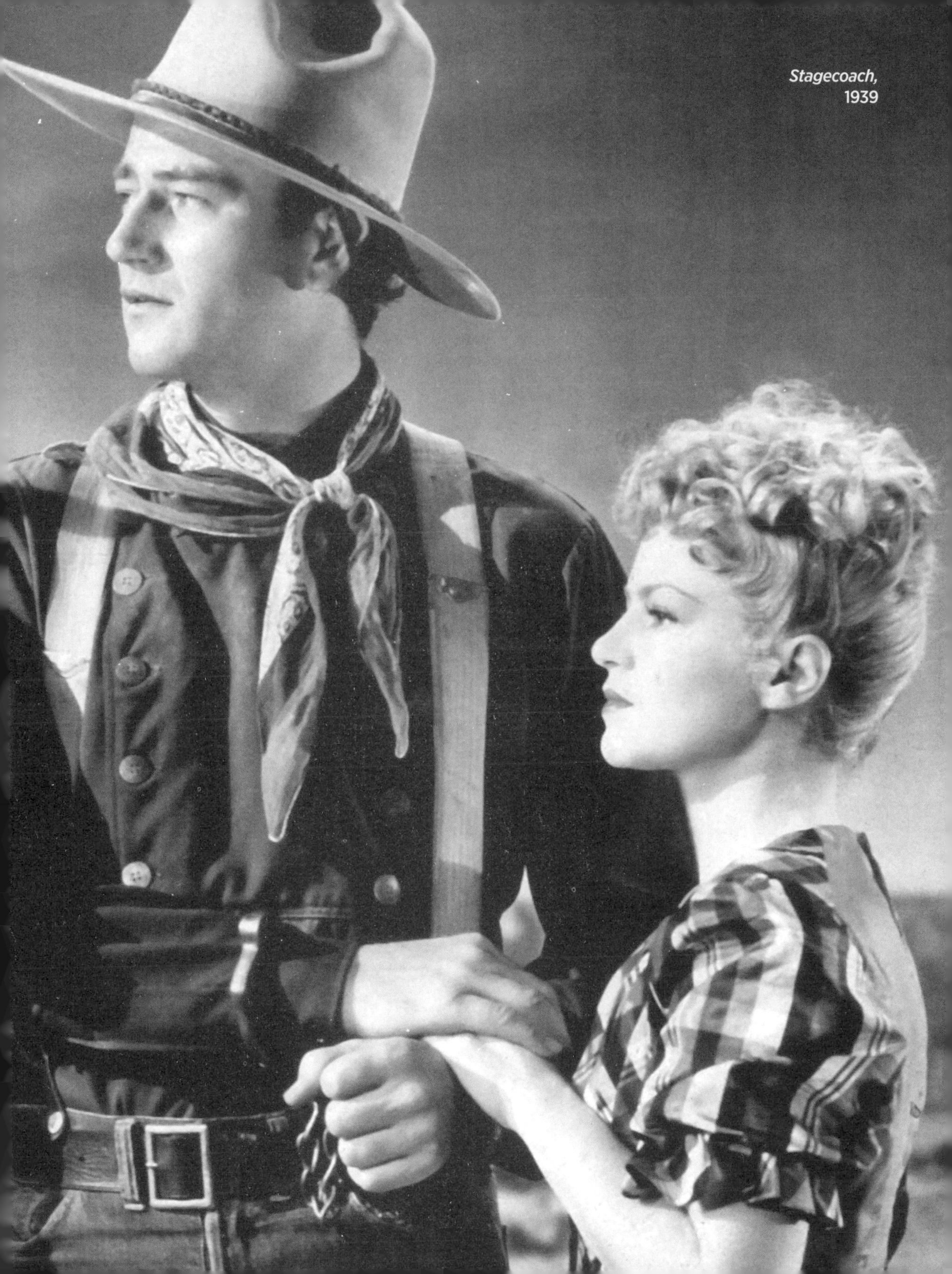

Stagecoach, 1939

John Wayne and a canine companion. Duke had many dogs as pets during his lifetime, including an Airedale terrier named Duke.

THE GREAT STATES

John Wayne was a patriot who loved his country more than anything. Prove your love of America by naming all 50 states!

1. _____
2. _____
3. _____
4. _____
5. _____
6. _____
7. _____
8. _____
9. _____
10. _____
11. _____
12. _____
13. _____
14. _____
15. _____
16. _____
17. _____

18. _____
19. _____
20. _____
21. _____
22. _____
23. _____
24. _____
25. _____
26. _____
27. _____
28. _____
29. _____
30. _____
31. _____
32. _____
33. _____
34. _____

35. _____
36. _____
37. _____
38. _____
39. _____
40. _____
41. _____
42. _____
43. _____
44. _____
45. _____
46. _____
47. _____
48. _____
49. _____
50. _____

LIKE FATHER, LIKE SON

Duke's son Patrick appeared in 10 movies with his father. Can you name them all?

1. _____

2. _____

3. _____

4. _____

5. _____

6. _____

7. _____

8. _____

9. _____

10. _____

John Wayne with son Patrick in one of the movies in which they both starred, 1950.

John Wayne and Ward Bond in one of their shared films (1956).

A CLOSE BOND

John Wayne and costar Ward Bond had a famously close friendship—
it's probably why they made so many films together! They made 22
in total, 14 of which came after Duke's big break in 1939. How many
of those last 14 films can you name?

1. _____

2. _____

3. _____

4. _____

5. _____

6. _____

7. _____

8. _____

9. _____

10. _____

11. _____

12. _____

13. _____

14. _____

COMMON COSTARS

John Wayne made two movies with Dean Martin and three with Lee Marvin.
Can you name them all?

DEAN MARTIN:

1. _____

2. _____

LEE MARVIN:

1. _____

2. _____

3. _____

Duke and Lee Marvin in one of their three shared films, 1963.

3 Godfathers, 1948.

★ ANSWER KEY

Check and see whether
you got it right.

WORD SEARCH
SOLUTIONS

PAGE 5

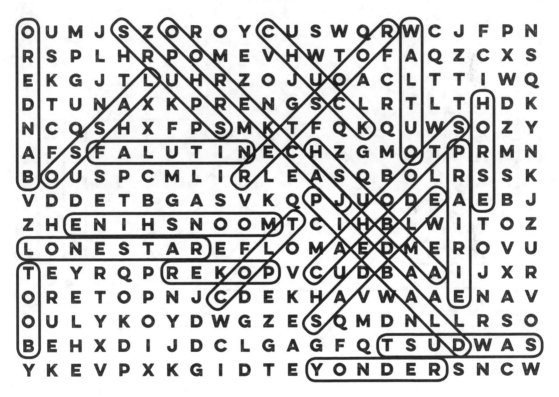

PAGE 7

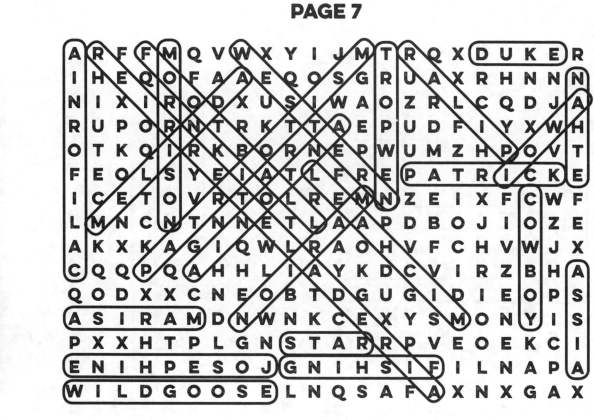

PAGE 8

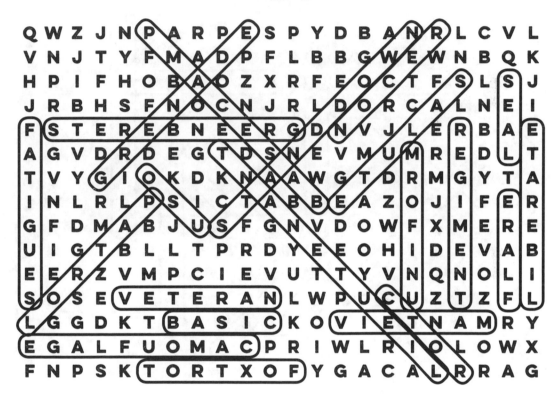

PAGE 11

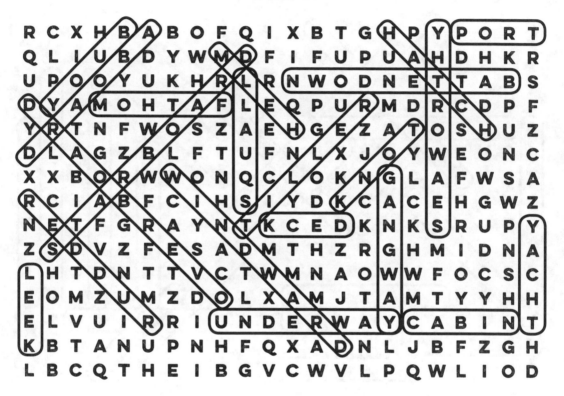

R C X H B A B O F Q I X B T G H P Y P O R T
Q L I U B D Y W M D F I F U P U A H D H K R
U P O O Y U K H R L R N W O D N E T T A B S
D Y A M O H T A F L E Q P U R M D R C D P F
Y R T N F W O S Z A E H G E Z A T O S H U Z
D L A G Z B L F T U F N L X J O Y W E O N C
X X B O R W W O N Q C L O K N G L A F W S A
R C I A B F C I H S I Y D K C A C E H G W Z
N E T F G R A Y N T K C E D K N K S R U P Y
Z S D V Z F E S A D M T H Z R G H M I D N A
L H T D N T T V C T W M N A O W W F O C S C
E O M Z U M Z D O L X A M J T A M T Y Y H H
E L V U I R R I U N D E R W A Y C A B I N T
K B T A N U P N H F Q X A D N L J B F Z G H
L B C Q T H E I B G V C W V L P Q W L I O D

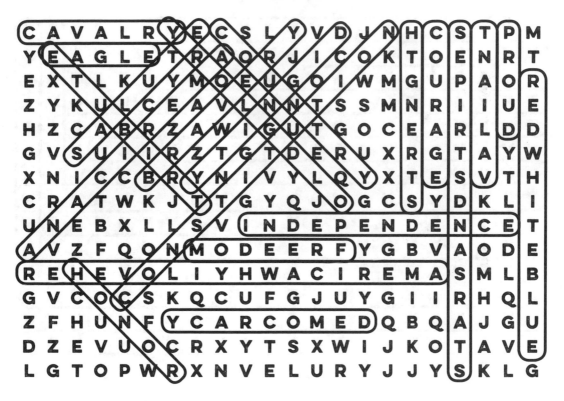

```
C A V A L R Y E C S L Y V D J N H C S T P M
Y E A G L E T R A O R J I C O K T O E N R T
E X T L K U Y M O E U G O I W M G U P A O R
Z Y K U L C E A V L N N T S S M N R I I U E
H Z C A B R Z A W I G U T G O C E A R L D D
G V S U I I R Z T G T D E R U X R G T A Y W
X N I C C B R Y N I V Y L Q Y X T E S V T H
C R A T W K J T T G Y Q J O G C S Y D K L I
U N E B X L L S V I N D E P E N D E N C E T
A V Z F Q O N M O D E E R F Y G B V A O D E
R E H E V O L I Y H W A C I R E M A S M L B
G V C O C S K Q C U F G J U Y G I I R H Q L U
Z F H U N F Y C A R C O M E D Q B Q A J G U
D Z E V U O C R X Y T S X W I J K O T A V E
L G T O P W R X N V E L U R Y J J Y S K L G
```

PAGE 14

```
W O H S N I T R A M N A E D E H T  K Q Q C C
E T U L A S W C H Z B W E Z R P I Q N T L A
N I A R T N O G A W Z R Q D E G L Z T G I S
T E X A C O S T A R T H E A T R E R G O M A
T H E D I C K P O W E L L T H E A T R E A B
K V A V G T H E B O B H O P E S H O W N X L
R U O H N O T L E K S D E R E H T H Z W S A
R O W A N A N D M A R T I N S L A U G H I N
S E I L L I B L L I H Y L R E V E B E H T C
E F I L R U O Y S I S I H T M A U D E D O A
A L C O A P R E M I E R E I L O V E L U C Y
D L R O W E D I W E D I W N O S N I K R A P
W H A T S M Y L I N E G U N S M O K E X F U
L H Q F D T H E E D S U L L I V A N S H O W
L W O H S S A L G U O D E K I M E H T M Y T
```

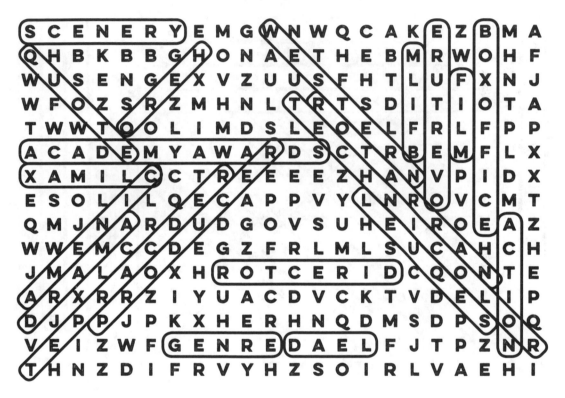

PAGE 19

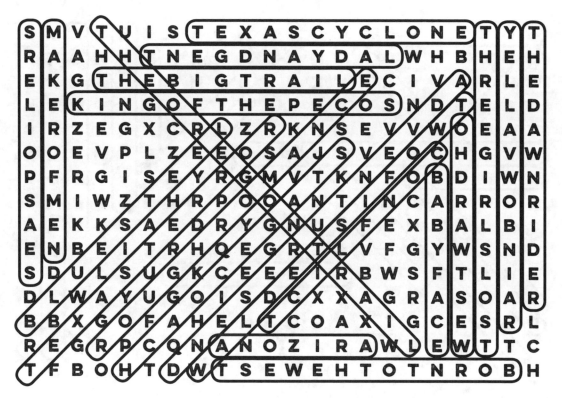

PAGE 20

PAGE 23

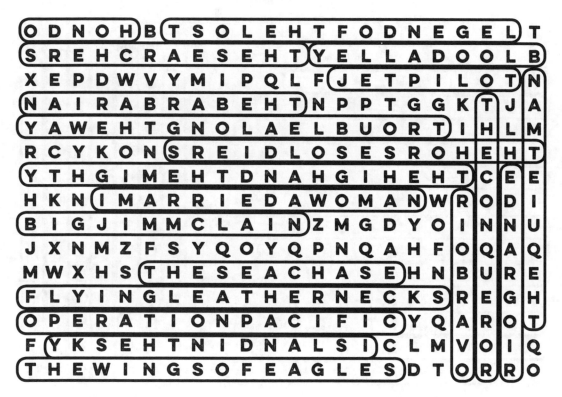

PAGE 24

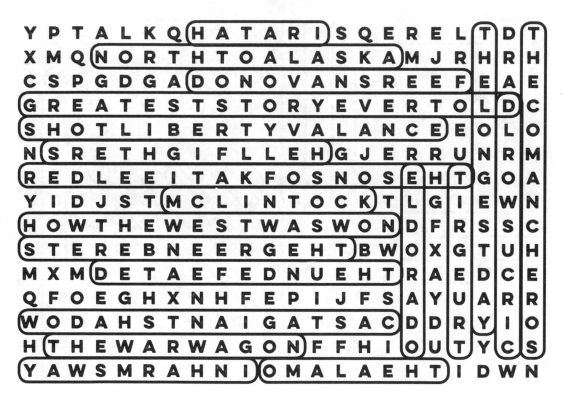

Y P T A L K Q H A T A R I S Q E R E L T D T
X M Q N O R T H T O A L A S K A M J R H R H
C S P G D G A D O N O V A N S R E E F E A E
G R E A T E S T S T O R Y E V E R T O L D C
S H O T L I B E R T Y V A L A N C E E O L O
N S R E T H G I F L L E H G J E R R U N R M
R E D L E E I T A K F O S N O S E H T G O A
Y I D J S T M C L I N T O C K T L G I E W N
H O W T H E W E S T W A S W O N D F R S S C
S T E R E B N E E R G E H T B W O X G T U H
M X M D E T A E F E D N U E H T R A E D C E
Q F O E G H X N H F E P I J F S A Y U A R R
W O D A H S T N A I G A T S A C D D R Y I O
H T H E W A R W A G O N F F H I O U T Y C S
Y A W S M R A H N I O M A L A E H T I D W N

PAGE 26

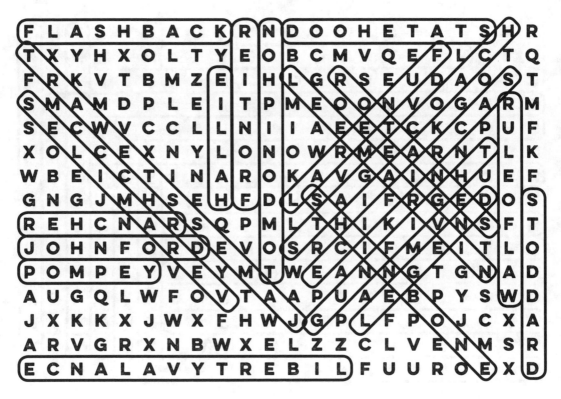

F L A S H B A C K R N D O O H E T A T S H R
T X Y H X O L T Y E O B C M V Q E F L C T Q
F R K V T B M Z E I H L G R S E U D A O S T
S M A M D P L E I T P M E O O N V O G A R M
S E C W V C C L L N I I A E E T C K C P U F
X O L C E X N Y L O N O W R M E A R N T L K
W B E I C T I N A R O K A V G A I N H U E F
G N G J M H S E H F D L S A I F R G E D O S
R E H C N A R S Q P M L T H I K I V N S F T
J O H N F O R D E V O S R C I F M E I T L O
P O M P E Y V E Y M T W E A N N G T G N A D
A U G Q L W F O V T A A P U A E B P Y S W D
J X K K X J W X F H W J G P L F P O J C X A
A R V G R X N B W X E L Z Z C L V E N M S R
E C N A L A V Y T R E B I L F U U R O E X D

PAGE 29

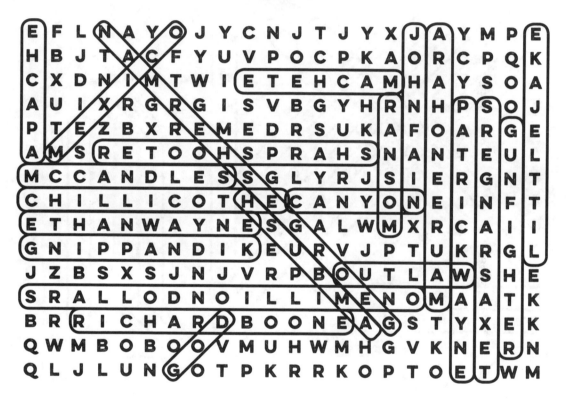

E F L N A Y O J Y C N J T J Y X J A Y M P E
H B J T A C F Y U V P O C P K A O R C P Q K
C X D N I M T W I E T E H C A M H A Y S O A
A U I X R G R G I S V B G Y H R N H P S O J
P T E Z B X R E M E D R S U K A F O A R G E
A M S R E T O O H S P R A H S N A T E U L T
M C C A N D L E S S G L Y R J S I E R G N T
C H I L L I C O T H E C A N Y O N E I N F I
E T H A N W A Y N E S G A L W M X R C A I L
G N I P P A N D I K E U R V J P T U K R G E
J Z B S X S J N J V R P B O U T L A W S H E
S R A L L O D N O I L L I M E N O M A A T K
B R R I C H A R D B O O N E A G S T Y X E K
Q W M B O B O O V M U H W M H G V K N E R N
Q L J L U N G O T P K R R K O P T O E T W M

PAGE 30

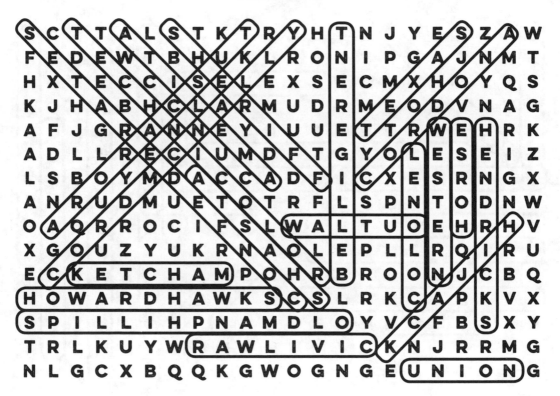

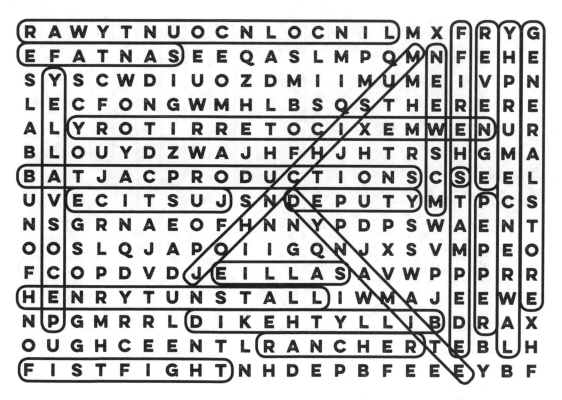

R A W Y T N U O C N L O C N I L M X F R Y G
E F A T N A S E E Q A S L M P Q M N F E H E
S Y S C W D I U O Z D M I I M U M E I V P N
L E C F O N G W M H L B S O S T H E R E R E
A L Y R O T I R R E T O C I X E M W E N U R
B L O U Y D Z W A J H F H J H T R S H G M A
B A T J A C P R O D U C T I O N S C S E E L
U V E C I T S U J S N D E P U T Y M T P C S
N S G R N A E O F H N N Y P D P S W A E N T
O O S L Q J A P O I I G Q N J X S V M P E O
F C O P D V D J E I L L A S A V W P P P R R
H E N R Y T U N S T A L L I W M A J E E W E
N P G M R R L D I K E H T Y L L I B D R A X
O U G H C E E N T L R A N C H E R T E B L H
F I S T F I G H T N H D E P B F E E Y B F

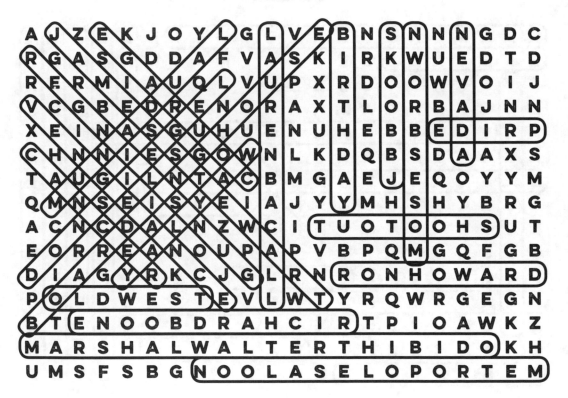

PAGE 37

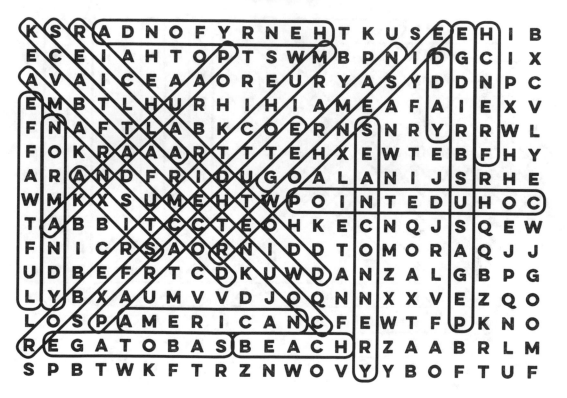

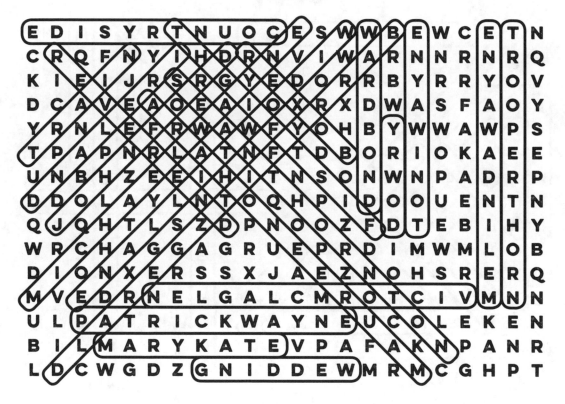

PAGE 41

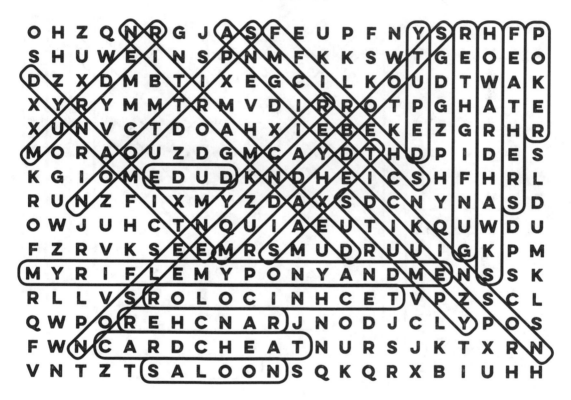

PAGE 42

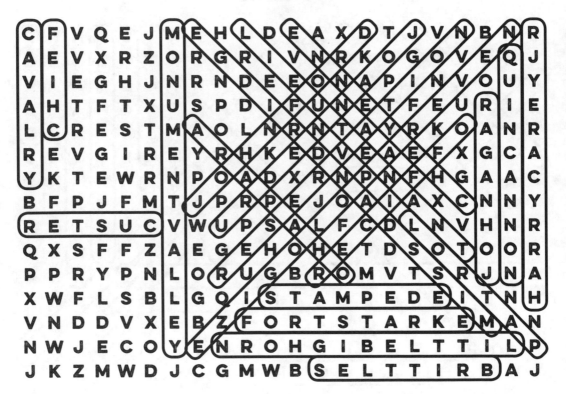

JUMBLES SOLUTIONS

PAGE 45
Out here, due process is a bullet!

PAGE 46
I've made over 250 pictures and have never shot a guy in the back. Change it.

PAGE 47
Young fella, if you're looking for trouble, I'll accommodate ya.

PAGE 49
Well, there are some things a man just can't run away from.

PAGE 50
Into each life a little rain must fall.

PAGE 51
I don't guess people's hearts got anything to do with a calendar.

PAGE 53
All I do is sell sincerity and I've been selling the hell out of that ever since I started.

PAGE 54
No great trail was ever built without hardship.

PAGE 55
I lose my appetite for 'em after the first couple 'a dozen.

PAGE 56
Pilgrim, you're gonna need a couple of stitches.

PAGE 59
Can you tell us who is the dirty stinkin' lowdown rat that shot our pa?

PAGE 60
Tomorrow is the most important thing in life.

PAGE 61
Well, those gold stars don't stand for good behavior.

PAGE 62
Never apologize. It's a sign of weakness.

PAGE 64
It isn't always being fast or even accurate that counts. It's being willing.

PAGE 65
You're short on ears and long on mouth.

PAGE 67
We brought nothing into this world and it's certain we can carry nothing out.

PAGE 68
I've got a touch of hangover, bureaucrat. Don't push me.

PAGE 70
You left a boy out there to do a man's job!

PAGE 71
Talk low, talk slow, and don't say too much.

PAGE 73
Where I come from we don't shoot horses when they get ornery; we tame 'em.

PAGE 74
Some men are like books written in a strange language.

PAGE 75
Sorry don't get it done, Dude.

PAGE 76
If I had known that I would have put that patch on 35 years earlier.

PAGE 78
Well I don't favor talking to vermin, but I'll talk to you just this once.

PAGE 79
I've been called a lot of things, but not 'comfortable.'

PAGE 81
I never shot nobody I didn't have to.

PAGE 82
It's payday, boys, come and get it!

PAGE 83
A fellow as ugly as you are probably couldn't get to first base without a fire.

PAGE 84
You got a breath on you like a hot mince pie.

PAGE 86
You're a blackguard, a liar,

a hypocrite and a stench in the nostrils of honest men.

PAGE 87
I don't like quitters, especially when they're not good enough to finish what they start.

PAGE 89
So from now on, I'm strictly a one man band!

PAGE 90
Slap some bacon on a biscuit and let's go! We're burnin' daylight!

PAGE 91
Snakes like you usually die of their own poison.

PAGE 92
Fear is just one of the many words I don't know the meaning of.

PAGE 94
I guess you can't break out of prison and into society in the same week.

PAGE 95
All battles are fought by scared men who'd rather be someplace else.

PAGE 97
Next time you shoot somebody, don't go near 'em till you're sure they're dead!

PAGE 98
Friend, you better get another line of work; this one sure don't fit your pistol.

PAGE 99
You gotta learn right and you gotta learn fast.

PAGE 100
A man oughta do what he thinks is best.

PAGE 102
Maybe losing that arm took some of the fight out of him.

PAGE 103
Whoa, take 'er easy there, Pilgrim.

PAGE 105
You can't give the enemy a break. Send him to hell.

PAGE 106
The sun and the moon change, but the army knows no seasons.

PAGE 107
There's right and there's wrong. You gotta do one or the other.

PAGE 108
I won't be wronged, I won't be insulted, and I won't be laid a hand on.

PAGE 110
We may have to be neighbors, but I don't have to be neighborly.

PAGE 111
I wouldn't make it a habit of calling me that, son.

PAGE 113
My hope and prayer is that everyone know and love our country for what she really is and what she stands for.

PAGE 114
Can't a man have a drink around this town in peace?

PAGE 115
But he must learn that a man's word to anything, even his own destruction, is his honor.

PAGE 117
Don't confuse sincerity of purpose with success.

PAGE 118
Words are what men live by...words they say and mean.

PAGE 119
Because no matter where people go, sooner or later there's the law.

PAGE 120
There's no more time for praying! Amen!

PAGE 122
Don't say it's a fine morning or I'll shoot ya.

PAGE 123
I am a demonstrative man, a baby picker-upper, a hugger and a kisser—that's my nature.

SPOT THE DIFFERENCE SOLUTIONS

PAGE 127

PAGE 131

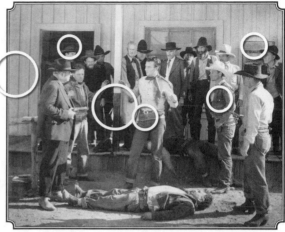

PAGE 129

PAGE 133

PAGE 135

PAGE 139

PAGE 137

PAGE 141

PAGE 143

PAGE 147

PAGE 145

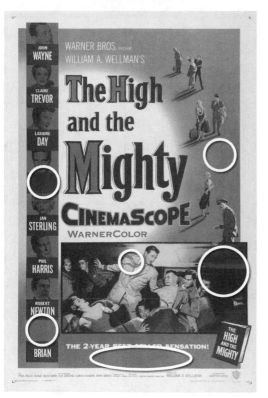

PAGE 149

PAGE 151

PAGE 155

PAGE 153

PAGE 157

PAGE 159

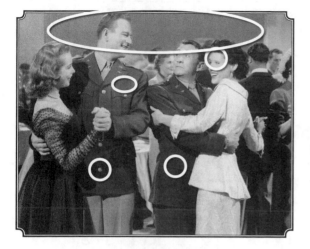

PAGE 163

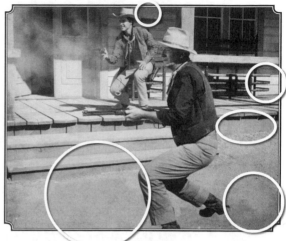

PAGE 161

PAGE 165

SU-DUKE-U SOLUTIONS

PAGE 167

6	4	2	5	7	9	3	1	8
1	9	3	4	8	2	7	6	5
8	5	7	1	3	6	4	9	2
4	2	1	6	5	3	8	7	9
3	6	9	8	1	7	5	2	4
5	7	8	2	9	4	1	3	6
9	3	6	7	4	8	2	5	1
2	1	4	3	6	5	9	8	7
7	8	5	9	2	1	6	4	3

PAGE 168

7	9	8	1	5	4	2	3	6
1	3	4	8	2	6	5	9	7
2	6	5	9	3	7	4	1	8
3	7	6	5	9	2	1	8	4
4	5	1	7	8	3	9	6	2
9	8	2	4	6	1	7	5	3
5	2	9	3	4	8	6	7	1
8	4	7	6	1	9	3	2	5
6	1	3	2	7	5	8	4	9

PAGE 169

1	4	8	3	6	7	2	5	9
3	9	7	2	5	4	8	1	6
5	6	2	8	1	9	7	3	4
6	7	5	1	3	2	9	4	8
9	8	3	5	4	6	1	2	7
4	2	1	7	9	8	3	6	5
8	1	6	9	2	5	4	7	3
2	5	9	4	7	3	6	8	1
7	3	4	6	8	1	5	9	2

PAGE 170

2	7	4	9	5	8	1	3	6
1	6	9	3	4	2	5	7	8
8	5	3	1	6	7	9	2	4
9	3	1	8	2	5	4	6	7
4	8	5	7	1	6	2	9	3
7	2	6	4	9	3	8	5	1
5	4	7	6	8	9	3	1	2
3	9	8	2	7	1	6	4	5
6	1	2	5	3	4	7	8	9

PAGE 171

6	4	9	7	5	1	8	3	2
2	1	7	8	3	6	5	9	4
3	5	8	4	9	2	7	6	1
7	9	2	1	6	8	3	4	5
8	3	1	5	7	4	9	2	6
4	6	5	9	2	3	1	7	8
9	7	4	6	1	5	2	8	3
1	8	3	2	4	9	6	5	7
5	2	6	3	8	7	4	1	9

PAGE 172

7	3	6	4	9	2	1	8	5
9	2	1	6	5	8	3	4	7
5	4	8	3	1	7	9	2	6
3	8	5	7	2	6	4	1	9
1	6	4	5	3	9	8	7	2
2	9	7	8	4	1	5	6	3
4	7	9	1	6	3	2	5	8
8	5	2	9	7	4	6	3	1
6	1	3	2	8	5	7	9	4

PAGE 173

8	4	5	3	7	9	1	2	6
9	3	7	6	1	2	4	5	8
2	1	6	4	8	5	3	7	9
7	2	1	8	9	3	6	4	5
3	5	8	1	6	4	7	9	2
4	6	9	2	5	7	8	3	1
6	9	3	5	4	1	2	8	7
5	8	2	7	3	6	9	1	4
1	7	4	9	2	8	5	6	3

PAGE 174

3	1	2	7	5	4	8	6	9
5	4	6	9	2	8	7	3	1
9	8	7	3	1	6	5	2	4
2	9	8	4	7	3	1	5	6
6	3	4	5	8	1	2	9	7
7	5	1	6	9	2	4	8	3
1	6	5	8	4	9	3	7	2
4	7	9	2	3	5	6	1	8
8	2	3	1	6	7	9	4	5

PAGE 175

4	5	2	1	9	3	6	8	7
8	9	1	6	5	7	2	4	3
3	7	6	8	2	4	1	9	5
9	2	4	5	6	8	7	3	1
7	6	3	9	4	1	5	2	8
5	1	8	3	7	2	9	6	4
6	3	7	4	1	9	8	5	2
2	8	5	7	3	6	4	1	9
1	4	9	2	8	5	3	7	6

PAGE 176

6	7	3	2	8	4	1	9	5
1	4	9	7	6	5	8	2	3
5	8	2	1	9	3	6	7	4
7	2	6	9	5	8	4	3	1
8	9	4	6	3	1	2	5	7
3	5	1	4	2	7	9	8	6
4	1	5	8	7	9	3	6	2
9	6	7	3	1	2	5	4	8
2	3	8	5	4	6	7	1	9

PAGE 177

2	1	4	8	6	5	3	7	9
8	7	6	9	1	3	5	2	4
5	9	3	4	2	7	6	1	8
6	5	2	7	3	9	4	8	1
9	8	7	1	5	4	2	6	3
3	4	1	6	8	2	9	5	7
4	6	9	2	7	1	8	3	5
1	3	8	5	9	6	7	4	2
7	2	5	3	4	8	1	9	6

PAGE 178

4	9	6	5	2	1	8	7	3
2	1	8	3	9	7	5	6	4
7	3	5	6	8	4	2	9	1
5	2	7	4	3	9	6	1	8
9	8	1	7	6	5	4	3	2
6	4	3	8	1	2	7	5	9
3	7	2	1	4	6	9	8	5
8	5	9	2	7	3	1	4	6
1	6	4	9	5	8	3	2	7

PAGE 179

1	2	5	6	4	9	7	3	8
9	6	4	3	7	8	1	2	5
3	7	8	5	2	1	9	6	4
4	9	1	8	3	7	6	5	2
2	5	3	1	6	4	8	9	7
6	8	7	9	5	2	4	1	3
8	3	2	7	9	6	5	4	1
5	1	9	4	8	3	2	7	6
7	4	6	2	1	5	3	8	9

PAGE 180

2	5	8	4	6	9	7	1	3
4	1	3	7	5	8	6	2	9
7	9	6	2	3	1	4	5	8
9	3	4	1	7	2	5	8	6
1	7	2	5	8	6	3	9	4
6	8	5	3	9	4	1	7	2
3	6	1	8	2	5	9	4	7
5	2	7	9	4	3	8	6	1
8	4	9	6	1	7	2	3	5

PAGE 181

5	8	2	9	1	3	6	7	4
6	4	7	2	8	5	3	1	9
3	1	9	4	6	7	2	8	5
7	5	8	3	2	9	4	6	1
9	6	3	8	4	1	7	5	2
1	2	4	7	5	6	8	9	3
8	3	6	1	9	2	5	4	7
4	7	1	5	3	8	9	2	6
2	9	5	6	7	4	1	3	8

PAGE 182

2	8	3	9	7	5	4	1	6
7	4	5	1	6	8	2	3	9
9	1	6	4	3	2	7	8	5
1	3	4	6	9	7	8	5	2
8	6	7	2	5	1	3	9	4
5	9	2	8	4	3	1	6	7
3	5	1	7	2	9	6	4	8
6	7	9	3	8	4	5	2	1
4	2	8	5	1	6	9	7	3

PAGE 183

7	3	6	8	4	2	9	5	1
4	2	1	3	5	9	6	7	8
8	9	5	6	1	7	4	2	3
3	8	9	7	2	5	1	4	6
5	6	4	1	8	3	7	9	2
1	7	2	9	6	4	8	3	5
2	4	8	5	9	6	3	1	7
6	5	3	4	7	1	2	8	9
9	1	7	2	3	8	5	6	4

PAGE 184

5	8	6	7	4	1	3	2	9
9	3	1	5	2	8	4	7	6
4	2	7	6	9	3	8	1	5
7	5	3	2	6	4	1	9	8
1	9	2	8	5	7	6	4	3
6	4	8	1	3	9	2	5	7
3	7	9	4	1	6	5	8	2
2	6	4	9	8	5	7	3	1
8	1	5	3	7	2	9	6	4

PAGE 185

2	5	9	1	3	4	6	7	8
7	8	3	2	6	5	1	9	4
4	6	1	9	7	8	5	3	2
8	7	6	4	2	1	3	5	9
9	3	2	7	5	6	8	4	1
5	1	4	3	8	9	2	6	7
1	4	8	6	9	3	7	2	5
6	9	7	5	1	2	4	8	3
3	2	5	8	4	7	9	1	6

PAGE 186

8	6	7	2	9	3	4	5	1
9	3	5	8	1	4	6	7	2
2	1	4	7	6	5	8	3	9
1	2	6	5	8	9	7	4	3
4	5	8	3	7	2	9	1	6
3	7	9	1	4	6	2	8	5
6	9	1	4	5	8	3	2	7
7	8	2	9	3	1	5	6	4
5	4	3	6	2	7	1	9	8

PAGE 187

4	5	2	7	6	1	9	3	8
6	9	1	5	3	8	7	4	2
7	8	3	4	9	2	6	5	1
9	3	5	1	2	6	8	7	4
1	2	7	9	8	4	5	6	3
8	4	6	3	5	7	1	2	9
5	1	4	2	7	9	3	8	6
3	6	9	8	4	5	2	1	7
2	7	8	6	1	3	4	9	5

PAGE 188

9	8	4	7	6	1	2	5	3
7	1	5	3	2	4	9	6	8
6	3	2	8	9	5	4	1	7
5	6	7	1	3	9	8	2	4
1	4	9	2	7	8	6	3	5
3	2	8	4	5	6	1	7	9
4	9	3	6	1	7	5	8	2
8	7	1	5	4	2	3	9	6
2	5	6	9	8	3	7	4	1

PAGE 189

8	3	2	4	9	7	6	1	5
5	1	7	2	6	8	3	4	9
9	6	4	3	1	5	7	2	8
1	2	9	5	7	6	4	8	3
3	4	6	8	2	9	5	7	1
7	8	5	1	3	4	9	6	2
2	5	8	6	4	3	1	9	7
6	9	3	7	8	1	2	5	4
4	7	1	9	5	2	8	3	6

PAGE 190

6	5	2	8	4	1	9	7	3
7	8	3	9	5	6	2	1	4
1	4	9	7	2	3	8	5	6
4	6	5	1	7	9	3	8	2
3	9	8	2	6	5	1	4	7
2	7	1	4	3	8	5	6	9
8	1	7	3	9	4	6	2	5
9	2	6	5	8	7	4	3	1
5	3	4	6	1	2	7	9	8

PAGE 191

5	1	8	7	2	3	9	6	4
2	9	4	6	1	5	8	3	7
7	6	3	4	8	9	2	5	1
3	2	9	8	4	6	7	1	5
8	4	5	1	9	7	3	2	6
6	7	1	5	3	2	4	8	9
9	5	6	2	7	8	1	4	3
1	3	2	9	5	4	6	7	8
4	8	7	3	6	1	5	9	2

PAGE 192

5	3	9	6	2	4	8	7	1
4	8	1	7	5	9	3	6	2
6	2	7	1	8	3	4	9	5
8	7	6	2	4	1	9	5	3
3	1	2	9	6	5	7	8	4
9	4	5	3	7	8	2	1	6
7	5	3	4	9	6	1	2	8
2	6	4	8	1	7	5	3	9
1	9	8	5	3	2	6	4	7

PAGE 193

4	2	3	1	9	7	6	5	8
8	5	1	6	2	4	9	7	3
6	7	9	8	3	5	2	4	1
2	9	8	4	6	1	7	3	5
5	1	6	2	7	3	8	9	4
3	4	7	9	5	8	1	6	2
7	3	2	5	8	6	4	1	9
1	8	5	7	4	9	3	2	6
9	6	4	3	1	2	5	8	7

PAGE 194

6	3	8	9	1	2	7	5	4
9	2	4	5	7	8	1	6	3
1	5	7	3	4	6	8	2	9
4	1	9	8	5	7	6	3	2
8	6	3	1	2	9	5	4	7
2	7	5	4	6	3	9	8	1
5	9	2	7	8	4	3	1	6
3	8	6	2	9	1	4	7	5
7	4	1	6	3	5	2	9	8

PAGE 195

5	4	7	6	2	8	9	3	1
9	8	6	1	3	5	7	4	2
2	3	1	4	7	9	6	5	8
8	1	2	5	9	6	4	7	3
3	6	4	2	1	7	8	9	5
7	5	9	8	4	3	1	2	6
4	7	8	3	5	1	2	6	9
6	2	5	9	8	4	3	1	7
1	9	3	7	6	2	5	8	4

PAGE 196

7	6	1	5	8	9	3	2	4
5	4	3	2	6	1	9	7	8
2	8	9	4	3	7	5	6	1
3	1	2	9	7	8	4	5	6
6	9	4	3	5	2	1	8	7
8	7	5	1	4	6	2	3	9
9	5	8	7	2	4	6	1	3
1	3	7	6	9	5	8	4	2
4	2	6	8	1	3	7	9	5

PAGE 197

6	2	3	9	4	5	1	8	7
1	9	4	7	8	6	2	3	5
7	5	8	3	2	1	6	4	9
9	7	1	5	6	4	8	2	3
5	8	2	1	9	3	7	6	4
4	3	6	8	7	2	5	9	1
8	4	9	6	5	7	3	1	2
3	6	7	2	1	9	4	5	8
2	1	5	4	3	8	9	7	6

PAGE 198

9	4	8	7	1	5	6	3	2
6	5	2	8	4	3	9	1	7
3	1	7	2	6	9	4	8	5
7	6	3	4	5	2	1	9	8
1	9	4	6	8	7	2	5	3
2	8	5	3	9	1	7	6	4
5	3	6	1	2	4	8	7	9
4	7	1	9	3	8	5	2	6
8	2	9	5	7	6	3	4	1

PAGE 199

5	1	2	6	4	8	7	9	3
8	3	6	7	2	9	4	1	5
9	4	7	3	1	5	8	6	2
4	2	8	5	9	6	1	3	7
3	5	9	4	7	1	6	2	8
7	6	1	8	3	2	5	4	9
1	9	4	2	8	7	3	5	6
2	7	5	1	6	3	9	8	4
6	8	3	9	5	4	2	7	1

PAGE 200

5	9	1	4	6	2	3	7	8
8	6	4	3	7	1	5	9	2
7	3	2	8	5	9	1	6	4
2	5	8	6	1	4	9	3	7
6	4	3	7	9	8	2	5	1
9	1	7	5	2	3	4	8	6
4	8	9	2	3	6	7	1	5
3	2	5	1	8	7	6	4	9
1	7	6	9	4	5	8	2	3

PAGE 201

4	2	7	8	1	6	9	3	5
1	6	5	4	9	3	8	2	7
9	8	3	5	2	7	6	4	1
5	7	8	1	3	9	4	6	2
6	1	2	7	4	8	3	5	9
3	9	4	2	6	5	7	1	8
7	5	1	3	8	4	2	9	6
2	3	9	6	7	1	5	8	4
8	4	6	9	5	2	1	7	3

PAGE 202

3	7	9	5	2	6	8	1	4
1	5	8	4	9	7	3	6	2
6	2	4	8	3	1	7	5	9
5	9	6	1	8	2	4	3	7
2	4	3	6	7	5	1	9	8
7	8	1	3	4	9	5	2	6
8	3	2	9	5	4	6	7	1
4	1	7	2	6	3	9	8	5
9	6	5	7	1	8	2	4	3

PAGE 203

3	1	8	2	6	7	4	5	9
5	6	4	1	3	9	2	7	8
9	2	7	5	8	4	6	3	1
1	7	2	8	5	3	9	6	4
6	3	9	4	7	2	1	8	5
4	8	5	6	9	1	3	2	7
7	4	3	9	2	8	5	1	6
8	5	1	3	4	6	7	9	2
2	9	6	7	1	5	8	4	3

PAGE 204

6	3	2	4	8	9	7	5	1
1	5	4	3	7	2	8	6	9
9	8	7	6	1	5	3	2	4
5	9	3	1	4	6	2	8	7
7	6	8	2	9	3	1	4	5
2	4	1	8	5	7	6	9	3
4	1	5	7	6	8	9	3	2
3	7	6	9	2	4	5	1	8
8	2	9	5	3	1	4	7	6

PAGE 205

3	1	4	5	2	7	6	9	8
6	7	8	1	9	4	5	3	2
5	2	9	8	3	6	7	4	1
1	9	6	7	8	2	4	5	3
4	5	3	9	6	1	2	8	7
7	8	2	3	4	5	1	6	9
2	3	1	6	5	9	8	7	4
9	4	5	2	7	8	3	1	6
8	6	7	4	1	3	9	2	5

PAGE 206

6	1	4	3	2	7	8	9	5
8	2	7	6	5	9	1	3	4
9	3	5	4	1	8	2	7	6
3	6	8	1	4	2	9	5	7
7	4	2	9	8	5	3	6	1
1	5	9	7	6	3	4	8	2
4	9	1	8	7	6	5	2	3
5	7	3	2	9	1	6	4	8
2	8	6	5	3	4	7	1	9

PAGE 207

3	1	6	4	5	8	7	9	2
8	4	9	7	2	6	5	3	1
7	5	2	3	1	9	4	8	6
6	8	5	2	9	7	3	1	4
2	3	1	5	8	4	9	6	7
9	7	4	1	6	3	8	2	5
5	9	8	6	4	2	1	7	3
4	2	7	9	3	1	6	5	8
1	6	3	8	7	5	2	4	9

PAGE 208

5	6	2	3	1	8	7	4	9
1	4	3	7	9	5	8	6	2
7	8	9	4	2	6	3	5	1
6	2	1	5	8	7	4	9	3
4	9	7	1	3	2	5	8	6
8	3	5	9	6	4	2	1	7
3	7	6	8	4	9	1	2	5
9	1	8	2	5	3	6	7	4
2	5	4	6	7	1	9	3	8

PAGE 209

1	4	7	3	6	8	2	5	9
6	5	3	1	9	2	4	7	8
8	2	9	5	7	4	1	6	3
4	8	5	9	2	6	3	1	7
2	9	1	8	3	7	6	4	5
7	3	6	4	5	1	9	8	2
3	1	2	6	8	5	7	9	4
5	7	4	2	1	9	8	3	6
9	6	8	7	4	3	5	2	1

PAGE 210

3	6	7	5	8	2	1	4	9
4	8	2	9	1	3	5	7	6
1	5	9	7	6	4	2	3	8
9	4	1	6	2	8	7	5	3
2	3	8	1	7	5	9	6	4
5	7	6	4	3	9	8	2	1
8	2	5	3	4	1	6	9	7
6	9	3	8	5	7	4	1	2
7	1	4	2	9	6	3	8	5

PAGE 211

9	7	1	5	8	3	4	6	2
3	5	2	4	7	6	1	9	8
6	8	4	2	9	1	7	3	5
4	1	3	9	6	8	2	5	7
7	2	8	3	5	4	9	1	6
5	9	6	7	1	2	3	8	4
2	6	7	8	3	9	5	4	1
8	4	9	1	2	5	6	7	3
1	3	5	6	4	7	8	2	9

PAGE 212

5	4	6	7	1	3	9	2	8
7	9	2	8	5	6	3	4	1
8	3	1	2	4	9	7	5	6
4	6	9	3	2	5	1	8	7
2	1	8	4	9	7	5	6	3
3	5	7	6	8	1	4	9	2
9	2	3	1	6	4	8	7	5
1	8	5	9	7	2	6	3	4
6	7	4	5	3	8	2	1	9

PAGE 213

3	4	2	5	6	7	1	9	8
8	9	1	3	2	4	7	5	6
7	6	5	8	1	9	3	2	4
1	3	4	9	7	6	5	8	2
5	8	9	2	3	1	4	6	7
2	7	6	4	5	8	9	1	3
9	5	3	6	4	2	8	7	1
4	2	7	1	8	5	6	3	9
6	1	8	7	9	3	2	4	5

PAGE 214

9	1	6	3	4	5	2	8	7
8	2	4	7	6	1	9	5	3
7	5	3	2	9	8	1	4	6
6	3	2	8	5	7	4	9	1
1	4	7	9	3	2	5	6	8
5	9	8	6	1	4	3	7	2
2	6	9	4	8	3	7	1	5
3	8	5	1	7	9	6	2	4
4	7	1	5	2	6	8	3	9

PAGE 215

2	3	9	4	1	8	6	5	7
5	4	1	3	7	6	9	2	8
7	8	6	9	5	2	1	3	4
6	9	3	2	4	5	7	8	1
1	7	2	6	8	3	5	4	9
8	5	4	7	9	1	3	6	2
4	1	5	8	3	9	2	7	6
9	2	8	5	6	7	4	1	3
3	6	7	1	2	4	8	9	5

PAGE 216

8	1	4	7	9	5	6	3	2
6	2	9	8	3	4	1	7	5
3	7	5	6	1	2	9	4	8
1	4	3	9	5	7	8	2	6
5	8	7	2	6	3	4	9	1
9	6	2	1	4	8	7	5	3
2	5	8	4	7	1	3	6	9
7	9	1	3	2	6	5	8	4
4	3	6	5	8	9	2	1	7

PAGE 217

3	5	2	9	1	8	4	7	6
8	6	7	3	2	4	1	9	5
9	1	4	7	6	5	3	2	8
2	8	6	4	9	3	5	1	7
7	9	1	8	5	6	2	3	4
4	3	5	2	7	1	8	6	9
5	2	8	6	3	9	7	4	1
6	4	3	1	8	7	9	5	2
1	7	9	5	4	2	6	8	3

PAGE 218

4	2	9	5	8	6	7	3	1
8	5	7	1	2	3	9	4	6
1	6	3	9	7	4	5	2	8
2	9	5	8	6	1	4	7	3
7	3	1	4	9	2	6	8	5
6	8	4	3	5	7	2	1	9
9	7	2	6	3	8	1	5	4
3	4	6	7	1	5	8	9	2
5	1	8	2	4	9	3	6	7

PAGE 219

5	2	4	3	9	7	1	8	6
9	1	6	2	8	4	5	7	3
3	8	7	6	5	1	2	9	4
6	3	9	7	1	2	8	4	5
1	7	8	5	4	3	9	6	2
2	4	5	9	6	8	3	1	7
7	9	2	1	3	6	4	5	8
8	6	1	4	2	5	7	3	9
4	5	3	8	7	9	6	2	1

PAGE 220

7	9	2	5	3	6	1	4	8
5	8	3	2	1	4	6	7	9
4	1	6	7	9	8	2	3	5
1	6	9	8	7	3	5	2	4
3	5	4	9	2	1	7	8	6
8	2	7	4	6	5	3	9	1
6	7	5	3	4	9	8	1	2
2	4	1	6	8	7	9	5	3
9	3	8	1	5	2	4	6	7

PAGE 221

4	9	5	2	6	8	7	1	3
6	2	1	9	7	3	5	4	8
8	7	3	5	4	1	9	2	6
2	8	7	6	9	4	1	3	5
9	3	6	1	5	2	4	8	7
1	5	4	3	8	7	6	9	2
5	6	2	4	3	9	8	7	1
3	4	8	7	1	5	2	6	9
7	1	9	8	2	6	3	5	4

PAGE 222

3	5	4	6	9	7	1	8	2
6	7	8	5	1	2	4	9	3
9	2	1	8	4	3	5	6	7
1	6	5	9	2	8	7	3	4
2	4	7	3	6	1	9	5	8
8	9	3	7	5	4	6	2	1
7	3	9	1	8	6	2	4	5
4	8	6	2	7	5	3	1	9
5	1	2	4	3	9	8	7	6

PAGE 223

3	1	5	7	8	2	9	6	4
8	6	7	1	4	9	2	5	3
9	4	2	5	6	3	1	7	8
7	5	1	6	9	4	8	3	2
2	8	6	3	7	1	5	4	9
4	3	9	8	2	5	6	1	7
6	9	3	2	5	7	4	8	1
5	7	4	9	1	8	3	2	6
1	2	8	4	3	6	7	9	5

PAGE 224

4	6	9	5	3	8	2	7	1
2	8	7	4	1	6	5	3	9
5	3	1	7	9	2	6	8	4
9	7	5	8	4	3	1	2	6
3	4	8	2	6	1	7	9	5
6	1	2	9	5	7	3	4	8
1	9	6	3	7	4	8	5	2
7	2	4	1	8	5	9	6	3
8	5	3	6	2	9	4	1	7

PAGE 225

3	6	2	7	5	4	8	1	9
7	8	1	9	3	2	4	5	6
9	4	5	8	6	1	2	3	7
2	7	3	4	1	5	9	6	8
4	5	8	6	9	3	7	2	1
1	9	6	2	7	8	3	4	5
6	3	7	1	4	9	5	8	2
8	1	4	5	2	7	6	9	3
5	2	9	3	8	6	1	7	4

CROSSWORDS SOLUTIONS

PAGE 229

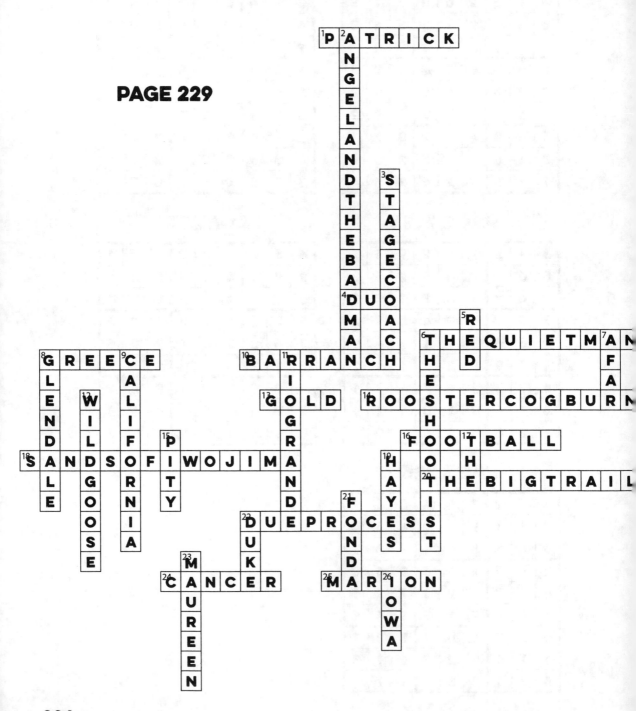

PAGE 231

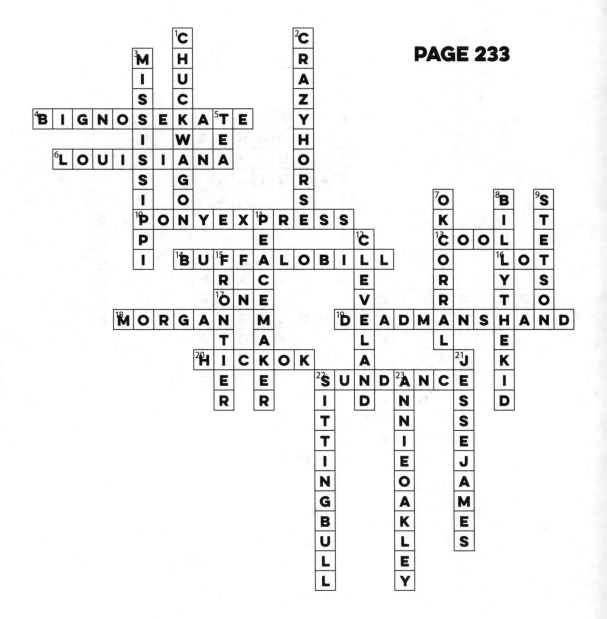

PAGE 233

PAGE 235

PAGE 237

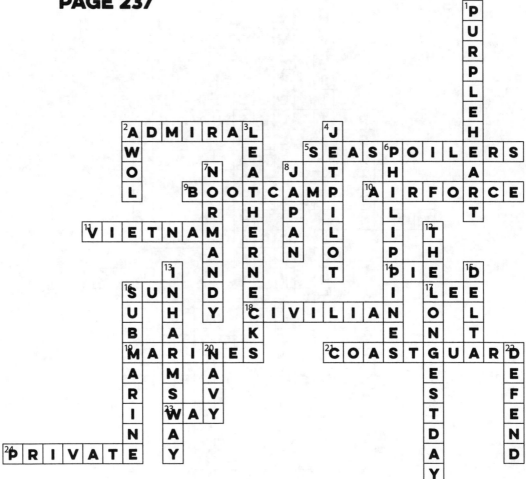

PAGE 239

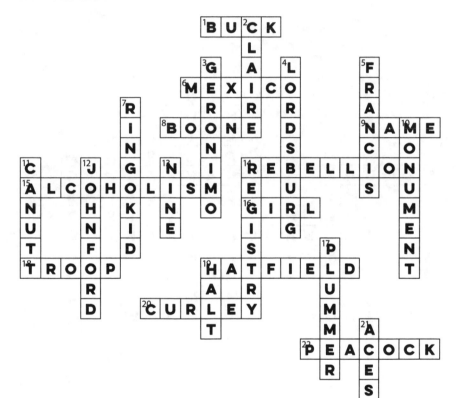

PAGE 241

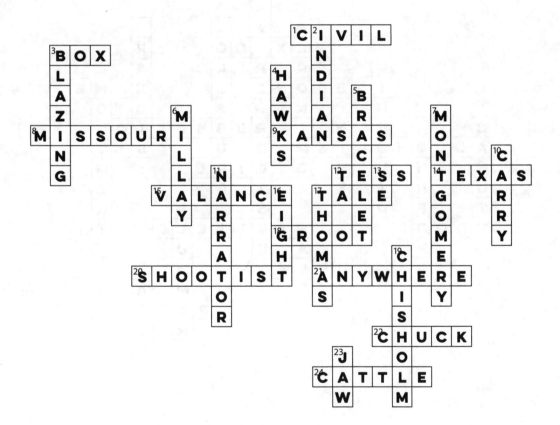

PAGE 243

PAGE 245

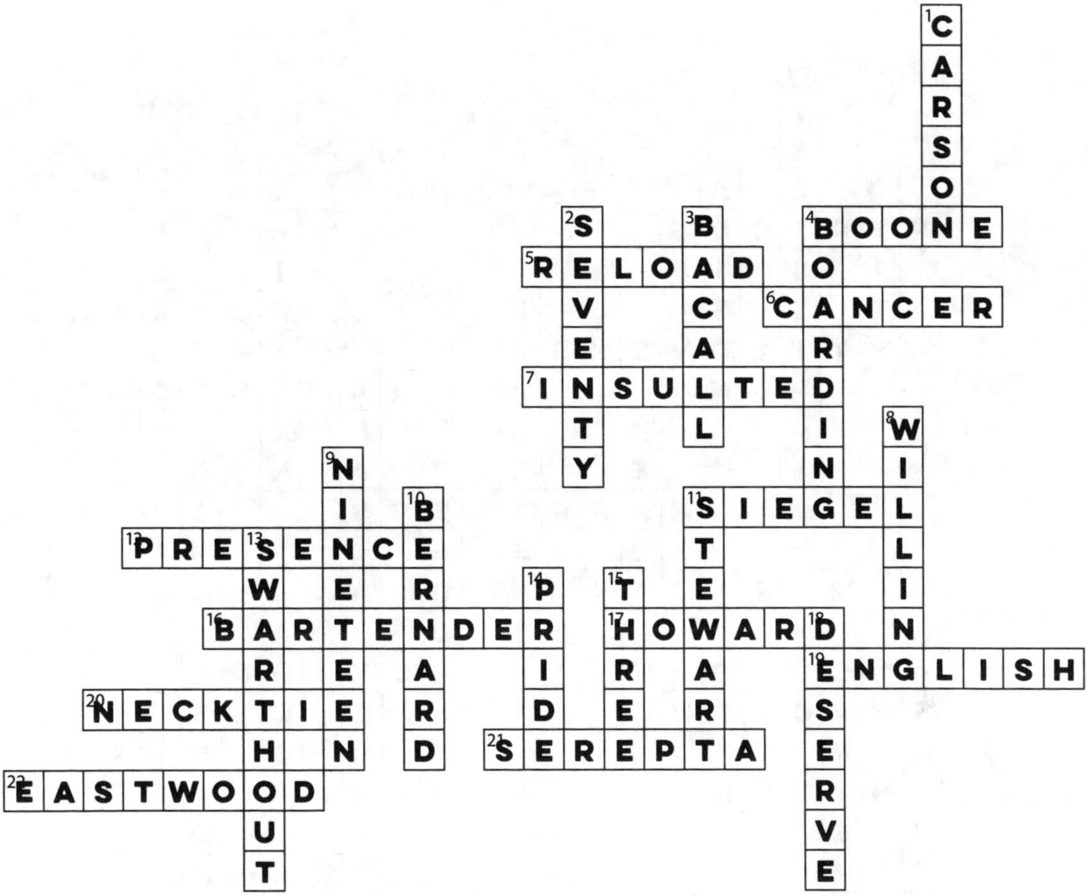
1 CARSON
2 SEVENTY
3 BACALL
4 BOONE
4 BOARDING
5 RELOAD
6 CANCER
7 INSULTED
8 WILLING
9 NINETEEN
10 BERNARD
11 SIEGEL
11 STEWART
12 PRESENCE
13 SWARTHOUT
14 PRIDE
15 THREE
16 BARTENDER
17 HOWARD
18 DESERVE
19 ENGLISH
20 NECKTIE
21 SEREPTA
22 EASTWOOD

PAGE 247

FINISH THE LIST SOLUTIONS

MOVIES WITH MAUREEN
Rio Grande (1950)
The Quiet Man (1952)
The Wings of Eagles (1957)
McLintock! (1963)
Big Jake (1971)

FAMILY MAN
Michael
Mary Antonia ("Toni")
Patrick
Melinda
Aissa
John Ethan
Marisa

ACADEMY AWARDS
Sands of Iwo Jima (1949)
The Alamo (1960)
True Grit (1969)

THE FINAL 10
Chisum (1970)
Rio Lobo (1970)
Big Jake (1971)
The Cowboys (1972)
The Train Robbers (1973)
Cahill U.S. Marshal (1973)
McQ (1974)
Brannigan (1975)
Rooster Cogburn (1975)
The Shootist (1976)

MILITIA MAN
1. Air Force
2. Army
3. Coast Guard
4. Marine Corps
5. Navy
Bonus
1. *Fort Apache* (1948)
2. *She Wore A Yellow Ribbon* (1949)
3. *Rio Grande* (1950)

9 STRANGE PEOPLE
1. Buck
2. Dallas
3. Doc Boone
4. Hatfield
5. Henry Gatewood
6. Henry the "Ringo Kid"
7. Lucy Mallory
8. Marshal Curley Wilcox
9. Samuel Peacock

THE GREAT STATES
1. Alabama
2. Alaska
3. Arizona
4. Arkansas
5. California
6. Colorado
7. Connecticut
8. Delaware
9. Florida
10. Georgia
11. Hawaii
12. Idaho
13. Illinois
14. Indiana
15. Iowa
16. Kansas
17. Kentucky
18. Louisiana
19. Maine
20. Maryland
21. Massachusetts
22. Michigan
23. Minnesota
24. Mississippi
25. Missouri
26. Montana
27. Nebraska
28. Nevada
29. New Hampshire
30. New Jersey
31. New Mexico
32. New York
33. North Carolina
34. North Dakota
35. Ohio
36. Oklahoma
37. Oregon
38. Pennsylvania
39. Rhode Island
40. South Carolina
41. South Dakota
42. Tennessee
43. Texas
44. Utah
45. Vermont
46. Virginia
47. Washington
48. West Virginia
49. Wisconsin
50. Wyoming

LIKE FATHER, LIKE SON
1. *Rio Grande* (1950)
2. *The Quiet Man* (1952)
3. *The Conqueror* (1956)
4. *The Searchers* (1956)
5. *The Alamo* (1960)
6. *The Comancheros* (1961)
7. *Donovan's Reef* (1963)
8. *McLintock!* (1963)
9. *The Green Berets* (1968)
10. *Big Jake* (1971)

A CLOSE BOND
1. *The Long Voyage Home* (1940)
2. *A Man Betrayed* (1941)
3. *The Shepherd of the Hills* (1941)
4. *Tall in the Saddle* (1944)
5. *Dakota* (1945)
6. *They Were Expendable* (1945)
7. *Fort Apache* (1948)
8. *3 Godfathers* (1948)
9. *Operation Pacific* (1951)
10. *The Quiet Man* (1952)
11. *Hondo* (1953)
12. *The Searchers* (1956)
13. *The Wings of Eagles* (1957)
14. *Rio Bravo* (1959)

COMMON COSTARS
Dean Martin:
1. *Rio Bravo* (1959)
2. *The Sons of Katie Elder* (1965)
Lee Marvin:
1. *The Comancheros* (1961)
2. *The Man Who Shot Liberty Valance* (1962)
3. *Donovan's Reef* (1963)